How to be a
BETTER
MANAGER

How to be a BETTER MANAGER

Michael Armstrong

Kogan
Page

First published in Great Britain in 1983
by Kogan Page Ltd
120 Pentonville Road
London N1 9JN

British Library Cataloguing in Publication Data

Armstrong, Michael
How to be a better manager.
1. Management
I. Title
658.4 HD31

ISBN 0-85038-638-1

Printed in Great Britain by Nene Litho,
bound by Woolnough Bookbinding
both of Wellingborough, Northants.

Contents

Introduction

The role of experience

'How can I become a better manager?' A familiar answer to this question is to say that 'managers learn to manage by managing under the guidance of a good manager'. But can experience alone be the best teacher? Several writers have expressed their doubts on this score. Tennyson called it 'a dirty nurse'. Oscar Wilde noted that 'experience is the name everyone gives to their mistakes'. And the historian Froude wrote that 'experience teaches slowly and at the cost of mistakes'.

Experience is an essential way of learning to improve but it is an imperfect instrument. We also need guidance — from a good manager *and* from other sources — which will help us to interpret experience, learn from our mistakes and make better use of our experience in the future.

The role of personality

'Managers are born not made.' This is the other rather discouraging answer given to the manager who seeks a way to improve himself. The implication that neither experience nor study can be beneficial is of course unacceptable, but the statement does contain some truth in that our personality strongly influences the way in which we manage and our effectiveness as a manager.

Studies carried out on the qualities displayed by successful top managers as quoted by Rosemary Stewart show a number of common characteristics, such as:

☐ Willingness to work hard, immensely hard in some cases
☐ Perseverance and determination, amounting at times to fanatical single-mindedness
☐ A willingness to take risks that are sometimes large gambles

9

☐ Ability to inspire enthusiasm in those whose cooperation and assistance are essential
☐ Toughness, amounting in some cases to ruthlessness.

Psychologists claim that personality is formed in the early years of life. Apparently, it is in the cradle, or at least in the nursery, that we learn to be ruthless. *If* this is the case, then maybe there is not much we can do about it when we grow up and become managers. Spending ten minutes every morning before a mirror practising being ruthless may not get us very far. Neither will much good come from our boss's exhortations to display different personality characteristics, or from attending lectures, or reading management textbooks. We can, however, modify the way in which we behave — the way in which we use our personalities. And guidance — not exhortations — from outside sources as well as from within should help. If we know what we are looking for we are more likely to find it.

What can be done?

Perhaps Francis Bacon provided the best answer to this question when he wrote: 'Studies perfect nature and are perfected by experience.'

The art of management — and it is an art — is important enough to be studied. The aim of these studies should be to help us to make better use of our personalities and intelligence and to ensure that past experience is better interpreted and more fully used, and that future experience is more quickly and purposefully absorbed.

There are three aspects of management which deserve to be considered in becoming a better manager:

☐ What management is about — an understanding of what knowledge and skills are required to be an effective manager
☐ Basic management techniques
☐ The skills managers use in managing people, getting results and applying techniques.

What management is about

Management is often said to be about getting things done through people or, in Rosemary Stewart's words: 'Deciding what should be done and getting other people to do it.' This definition emphasizes the 'people' aspect of management and therefore the art or skills of leadership, motivation, delegation, organization, etc.

The following definition by Frederick Hooper pays more attention to the 'doing' aspect of management and to the manager's responsibility for achieving the effective use of all resources — money, methods and materials as well as manpower:

> The task of management is to carry policy into effect with the fullest efficiency within the limits assigned: that is, with the maximum success at the minimum cost. Management aims to create conditions which will bring about the optimum use of all resources available to the undertaking in the form of men, methods and materials.

The process of management essentially consists of four functions:

Planning — deciding on a course of action to achieve a desired result. Plans focus attention on objectives and standards and the programmes required to achieve the objectives.

Organizing — setting up and staffing the most appropriate organization to achieve the aim.

Motivating — exercising leadership in order to motivate people to work to the best of their ability and smoothly together as part of a team.

Controlling — measuring and monitoring the progress of work in relation to the plan and taking corrective action when required.

Knowledge of management techniques

All managers start with the specialist, technical or professional knowledge which has brought them into their particular organization. On top of this they acquire and develop the management techniques which help them to carry out the four processes of management mentioned above. These techniques include appraising people, conducting interviews and improving productivity.

The manager also requires a knowledge of the environment in which he operates, and this involves such factors as the effects of organizational change, conflict, motivation, power and politics.

Managerial skills

The manager's skills include clear thinking, creativity, delegating, exercising leadership, and so on.

Use of this book

If you want to be a better manager your first task is to analyse yourself and work out those areas where you think improvement is required — on the basis of experience and, if it is available, the advice of your boss or colleagues.

This book deals individually with each of the management functions and with all the techniques and skills required of the manager. Subjects are dealt with in alphabetical order for ease of reference. Although no book can contain all the answers, it is hoped that you will find under one or more headings the foundation on which to build your managerial knowledge and skills.*

---

* Masculine pronouns have been used for convenience and conciseness, though feminine pronouns are, in most cases, equally applicable.

Chapter 1
Achieving results

Achieving results, getting things done, making things happen. That is what management is all about.

It can be said that there are three sorts of managers: those who make things happen, those who watch things happening, and those who don't know what is happening. Before finding out how to get into the first category, there are three questions to answer:

□ Is getting things done simply a matter of personality — characteristics like drive, decisiveness, leadership, ambition — which some people have and others haven't?

□ And if you haven't got the drive, decisiveness and so forth which it takes, is there anything you can do about it?

□ To what extent is an ability to make things happen a matter of using techniques which can be learnt and developed?

Personality is important. Unless you have willpower and drive nothing will get done. But remember that your personality is a function of both nature and nurture. You are born with certain characteristics. Upbringing, education, training and, above all, experience, develop you into the person you are.

We may not be able to change our personality which, according to Freud, is formed in the first few years of life. But we can develop and adapt it by consciously learning from our own experience and by observing and analysing other people's behaviour.

Techniques for achieving results, such as planning, organizing, delegating, communicating, motivating and controlling, can be learnt. These are dealt with later in this book. But these techniques are only as effective as the person who uses them. They must be applied in the right way and in the right circumstances. And you still have to use your experience to select the right technique, and your personality to make it work.

To become a person who makes things happen you therefore have to develop skills and capacities by a process of understanding, observation, analysis and learning. The four actions you should take are:

1. Understand what makes achievers tick — the personality characteristics they display in getting things done.
2. Observe what achievers do — how they operate, what techniques they use.
3. Analyse your own behaviour (*behaviour*, not personality), compare it with that of high achievers, and think how to improve your effectiveness.
4. Learn as much as you can about the management techniques available.

What makes achievers tick?

David McClelland of Harvard University carried out extensive research into what motivates managers. He interviewed, observed and analysed numbers of managers at their place of work and recorded findings, before producing his theory. And before you dismiss anything which comes under the heading of theory, remember what Douglas McGregor of the Massachusetts Institute of Technology, said: 'There is nothing so practical as a good theory.'

McClelland identified three needs which he believes are key factors in motivating managers. These are:

☐ The need for achievement
☐ The need for power (having control and influence over people)
☐ The need for affiliation (to be accepted by others).

All effective managers have these needs to a certain degree, but by far the most important one is achievement.

Achievement is what counts and achievers, according to McClelland, have these characteristics:

☐ They set themselves realistic but achievable goals with some 'stretch' built in.
☐ They prefer situations which they themselves can influence rather than those on which chance has a large influence.
☐ They are more concerned with knowing they have done

well than with the rewards that success brings.

☐ They get their rewards from their accomplishment rather than from money or praise. This does not mean that high achievers reject money, which does in fact motivate them as long as it is seen as a realistic measure of their performance.

☐ High achievers are most effective in situations where they are allowed to get ahead by their own efforts.

What do achievers do?

High achievers do some, if not all, of these things:

1. They define to themselves precisely what they want to do.
2. They set demanding but not unattainable time scales in which to do it.
3. They convey clearly what they want done and by when.
4. They are prepared to discuss how things should be done and will listen to and take advice. But once the course of action has been agreed they stick to it unless events dictate a change of direction.
5. They are single-minded about getting where they want to go, showing perseverance and determination in the face of adversity.
6. They demand high performance from themselves and are somewhat callous in expecting equally high performance from everyone else.
7. They work hard and work well under pressure; in fact, it brings out the best in them.
8. They tend to be dissatisfied with the status quo.
9. They are never completely satisfied with their own performance and continually question themselves.
10. They will take calculated risks.
11. They snap out of setbacks without being personally shattered and quickly re-group their forces and their ideas.
12. They are enthusiastic about the task and convey their enthusiasm to others.
13. They are decisive in the sense that they are able quickly to sum up situations, define alternative courses of action, determine the preferred course, and convey to their subordinates what needs to be done.
14. They continually monitor their own and their subordinates' performance so that any deviation can be corrected in good time.

How to analyse your own behaviour

It is no good trying to analyse your own behaviour unless you have criteria against which you can measure your performance. You have to set standards for yourself, and if you don't meet them, ask yourself why. The answer should tell you what to do next time.

The basic questions you should ask yourself are:

☐ What did I set out to do?
☐ Did I get it done?
☐ If I did, why and how did I succeed?
☐ If not, why not?

The aim is to make effective use of your experience.

Use the list of things that high achievers do to check your own behaviour and actions. If your performance has not been up to scratch under any of these headings, ask yourself specifically what went wrong and decide how you are going to overcome this difficulty next time. This is not always easy. It is hard to admit to yourself, for example, that you have not been sufficiently enthusiastic. It may be even harder to decide what to do about it. You don't want to enthuse all over the place, indiscriminately. But you can consider whether there are better ways of displaying and conveying your enthusiasm to others in order to carry them with you.

Learning

There are a number of management techniques that you need to know about. These techniques are discussed in subsequent chapters in this book. The ones you should be particularly interested in are:

☐ planning
☐ objective and target setting
☐ decision making
☐ delegating
☐ communicating
☐ motivating
☐ leadership
☐ coordinating
☐ controlling.

16

Conclusion

This process of observation, analysis and learning will help you become an achiever. But remember, achieving results is ultimately about making promises — to others and to yourself — and keeping them. Robert Townsend, in his book *Up the Organization*, had some excellent advice: 'Promises: keep. If asked when you can deliver something ask for time to think. Build in a margin of safety. Name a date. Then deliver it earlier than you promised.'

Chapter 2
Appraising people

A manager, it is said, is someone who gets things done through people. If you have people working for you, your results will depend largely on how well they do. You need to do whatever you can to improve their performance. You will do this if you:

1. Clarify responsibilities
2. Define and agree targets and standards of performance
3. Improve motivation by increasing understanding of goals, the means of attaining those goals and the rewards associated with their achievement
4. Provide guidance and help which will develop strengths and overcome weaknesses
5. Detect problems and difficulties and agree how to overcome them
6. Plan whatever training and development are needed.

The information required to do these things is provided by performance appraisal. You cannot manage people effectively, which means you cannot be an effective manager, unless you assess what they are doing and how they do it.

Two questions need to be answered:

☐ What overall approach do you adopt?
☐ What techniques, if any, do you use?

Overall approach

Every time anyone does anything for you, an impression will be formed in your mind of how well or how badly it has been done. The accumulation of these impressions provides you with your overall view about the individual's performance and potential. Your appraisal of staff will therefore be a continuous, although probably an intuitive, process. You may think this is enough, but is it? Challenge your assumption by answering the following questions:

☐ Am I certain that I do not place too much emphasis on recent evidence of good or indifferent performance, thus ignoring, or at least underestimating, the accumulated evidence of past performance?

☐ Do I really know the circumstances under which the work has been done, ie the extent to which it has been influenced by luck rather than management, or by factors beyond the individual's control?

☐ Can I really be sure that my judgements are not affected by my prejudices concerning personality or physical characteristics? Do I, for example, favour the showy extravert and underestimate the quiet plodder who still gets things done?

☐ Am I confident that I have not contributed to the failure by not clearly defining what I expected or by not giving the individual the scope, support, guidance and resources he needed?

It is a rare person who can honestly answer all those questions satisfactorily. For those who are less confident, a more systematic approach to appraisal should be considered. This should not involve elaborate and time-consuming techniques with a lot of paperwork. As in all other techniques of management, the motto is 'keep it simple'.

Appraisal techniques

The purpose of appraisal is to improve the performance of your staff by providing objective information on how they are doing, and which areas of their work require attention.

Remember that the emphasis should be to build on strengths as well as to overcome weaknesses.

The traditional method of appraising staff was to assess the individual once or perhaps twice a year against a list of personality characteristics. Grades or points were scored against each factor, and to help managers grade their staff guidelines were often provided.

It was Douglas McGregor, in a famous article in the *Harvard Business Review* entitled 'An Uneasy Look at Performance Appraisal', who exposed the real weakness of this method. First, he emphasized that an appraisal was useless unless the

HOW TO BE A BETTER MANAGER

results could be conveyed by the manager to his subordinate in a way which would motivate the latter to improve his performance. Second, he pointed out that managers did not like 'playing God' by criticizing subordinates on the basis of abstractions and generalities. Thirdly, he noted that the effectiveness of the communication from the manager to the subordinate is inversely related to the latter's need to hear it. The more serious the criticism, the less likely is the subordinate to accept it.

McGregor went on to stress that these problems are greatly increased when comments are centred on personality characteristics such as energy, initiative and willingness. The manager usually cannot substantiate his judgements and the subordinate automatically resents and probably rejects any criticism of himself as a person. Even where the manager tries to give concrete illustrations, he is likely to find himself on the defensive as the subordinate attempts to show that there are extenuating circumstances surrounding any illustration which is brought up.

Management by objectives

McGregor's answer to these problems was the concept of management by objectives first launched by Peter Drucker in 1954. The aim of management by objectives is to shift appraisal from personality to performance. It is a system whereby managers agree objectives with their subordinates and then review results against those objectives.

In *The Practice of Management*, Drucker explained the philosophy of management by objectives as follows:

> An effective management must direct the vision and efforts of all managers towards a common goal. It must ensure that the individual manager understands what results are demanded of him. It must ensure that the superior understands what to expect of each of his subordinate managers. It must motivate each manager to maximum efforts in the right direction. And while encouraging high standards of workmanship, it must make them the means to the end of business performance rather than the ends in themselves.

The essence of management by objectives is the commonsense proposition that if people know where to go they are more likely to get there. Add to this the idea that people will be more keen to do something if they have thought it out for themselves rather than having it imposed upon them, and the picture is complete.

Management by objectives therefore requires a manager and his subordinate to:

1. Agree on the targets and standards of performance the subordinate should achieve
2. Review results against the targets or standards and agree where improvements are needed and how they should be achieved
3. Agree new targets or standards.

Unfortunately, management by objectives became a sort of cult, supported by mounds of paper. Managers tried to quantify objectives which were clearly unquantifiable, especially in staff positions. In attempting to counsel people in the periodical reviews, managers did more to demotivate than to motivate them. Few managers, as McGregor said, are competent to practise psychotherapy. Many managers dislike formal appraisals and feel they are a waste of time. In these circumstances the task is unlikely to be conducted in a way which will encourage the subordinate to become more effective.

Furthermore, management by objectives failed because it became an annual ritual imposed upon unconvinced line managers by personnel managers and management consultants with axes to grind and techniques to sell. The idea that performance appraisal should be a natural and continuous process was lost in a welter of forms and procedures.

The task-centred method

The task-centred method relates to what the individual is actually doing and how he does it. It takes from management by objectives the concept of agreed targets, but it rejects the idea of formal periodical review as a means of helping people to learn how to improve their performance. In McGregor's words:

> The semi-annual or annual appraisal is not a particularly efficient stimulus to learning. It provides feedback about behaviour at a time remote from the behaviour itself. People do learn and change from feedback. In fact, it is the only way they learn. However, the most effective feedback occurs immediately after the behaviour. The subordinate can learn a great deal from a mistake, or a particular failure in performance, provided it is analysed while all the evidence is immediately at hand.

You should therefore appraise your staff by carrying out continuing reviews of how well agreed tasks have been completed. Provide guidance on where and how to improve as and when required. Encourage your subordinate to think for himself what should be done. Don't impose things on him unless you have to.

Avoid personality assessments. Concentrate on the task and how the task has been done. Sit back now and again and carry out a stock-taking exercise, reflecting on your own how well each of your subordinates is doing. Summarize your conclusions if you like — but on one side of one sheet of blank paper, not on a form. If the personnel department compels you to complete their pet form, do so. Send it to them and forget about it. They will.

Don't carry out a formal interview after this stock-taking exercise. Most people do it badly and you are likely to do more harm than good. But in the normal course of work, when the opportunity arises, discuss briefly and informally with your subordinate any points you wish to make. Give praise where praise is due, but also get your subordinate to agree on any things he needs to do to improve.

Performance appraisal then becomes a natural part of the process of management, not a technique foisted on you by someone else. It is a way of motivating, training and developing staff rather than an artificial rigmarole which too often produces the opposite effect to that which was intended.

A case study

To appraise people properly you need to know what you are appraising and convey that knowledge to your subordinate. In the *Harvard Business Review*, Harry Levinson told the story of a corporate president who put a senior executive in charge of a failing operation.

His only directive was 'Get it in the black'. Within two years of that injunction, the new executive moved the operation from a deficit position to one that showed a profit of several million. Fresh from his triumph the executive announced himself as a candidate for a higher-level position, and indicated that he was already receiving offers from other companies.

The corporate president however did not share the executive's positive opinions of his behaviour. In fact, the president was not at all pleased with the way the executive had handled things. Naturally the executive was dismayed and when he asked what he had done wrong, the corporate president told him that he had indeed accomplished what he had been asked to do, but he had done it singlehandedly, by the sheer force of his own personality. Furthermore, the executive was told, he had replaced people whom the company thought to be good employees with those it regarded as compliant. In effect, by demonstrating his own strength, he had made the organization weaker. Until the executive changed his authoritarian manner, his boss said, it was unlikely that he would be promoted further.

Implicit in this vignette is the common major fault in performance appraisal and management by objectives — namely, a fundamental misconception of what is to be appraised.

Chapter 3
Budgeting

The need for budgets

Budgets don't win friends but they do influence people. They can be painful to create and agonizing to manage. But they do translate policy into financial terms and, whether we like it or not, that is the way in which plans must be expressed and, ultimately, performance controlled.

Budgets are needed for three reasons:

- ☐ To show the financial implications of plans
- ☐ To define the resources required to achieve the plans
- ☐ To provide a means of measuring, monitoring and controlling results against the plans.

Limitations of budgets

The main problems in budgeting are:

- ☐ An inadequate basic budgeting procedure: imprecise guidelines, unsatisfactory background data, cumbersome systems, lack of technical advice and assistance to managers, arbitrary cuts by top management
- ☐ An unskilled or cynical approach by managers to budgeting, resulting from inadequate basic procedures, lack of guidance, training or encouragement, or a feeling that budgets are simply weapons to be deployed against them, rather than tools for them to use
- ☐ Lack of accurate forecasts of future activity levels
- ☐ Difficulty in amending the budget in response to changing circumstances
- ☐ The fundamental weakness of basing budgets on past levels of expenditure which are simply 'plussed up' rather than subjecting the whole of the budget to a critical examination

☐ Weaknesses in reporting or controlling procedures which prevent the budget being used to monitor performance.

Preparing budgets

Most of the problems concerning the preparation of budgets mentioned above can be reduced if not eliminated if the following steps are taken.

1. Prepare budget guidelines which set out policies on where you want to go and, broadly, how you want to get there. These could be expressed as targets, for sales production or activity levels, and as an outline of the major marketing and production plans. In addition, the assumptions to be used in budgeting should be given. These could include rates of inflation and increases in costs and prices.
2. Ensure that those responsible for preparing budgets are given advice and encouragement by management accountants. These experts should be there to help, not to prod or threaten.
3. Get people to think hard about their budgets. They should not be allowed just to update last year's actuals. Wherever there is any choice on how much is spent, they should be asked to go back to first principles and justify what they are doing (zero-base budgeting).
4. Do not accept any significant increase or even decrease from last year's budget without an explanation.
5. Probe to ensure that budgets submitted to you are realistic and do not include a 'fudge factor'.
6. Do not slash budgets arbitrarily. Give reasons. If you don't, you will get 'fudge factors' or a couldn't-care-less attitude.
7. Update or 'flex' budgets regularly, especially when activity levels and costs are subject to large variations.

Zero-base budgeting

The traditional approach to budgeting tends to perpetuate the commitments of previous years. For instance, past levels of expenditure are used as a base from which to project increases or decreases. Only part of the budget is analysed, and managers concentrate on justifying increases, rather than challenging the need for any function or activity in its present form.

Zero-base budgeting requires budget managers systematically

to re-evaluate all their activities and programmes in order to decide whether they should be eliminated, or funded at a reduced, similar, or increased level. (Direct labour need not be included if standard costs are used.) Appropriate funding levels will be determined by the priorities established by top management and the overall availability of funds.

Each activity is broken down into defined decision units, and each unit is analysed to establish:

- ☐ Its objectives
- ☐ The activities carried out
- ☐ The present costs of these activities
- ☐ The benefits resulting from each activity
- ☐ The standards and other performance measures that exist
- ☐ Alternative ways of achieving objectives
- ☐ Priorities among the objectives
- ☐ The advantages and disadvantages of incurring different levels of expenditure.

This is a fairly exhaustive list, and the amount of detail you want to pursue will depend on the importance you attach to a rigorous examination of expenditure. Zero-base budgeting is no panacea and it has often failed because companies have introduced over-elaborate procedures which have sunk almost without trace in a sea of paperwork. But the approach is right: cost control is about challenging and justifying proposed expenditures as well as monitoring what has actually been spent. The most elaborate control system in the world is useless if its foundation is unsound. Zero-base budgeting techniques should be used by managers to develop an attitude of mind in which they examine and control all their activities. The techniques should not be used in a threatening way. The emphasis should be on their value in getting priorities right and ensuring that costs and benefits are thoroughly reviewed to the advantage of all concerned.

Flexible budgets

If it is possible, with a reasonable degree of accuracy, to relate changes in income and costs to levels of activity, the use of flexible budgets is worthwhile. Budgets are 'flexed' by recalculating income and costs which vary with activity levels by reference to actual activity levels, thus giving an 'expected' level of income and costs. The difference between the original and expected levels is termed an 'activity variance' and the difference between expected levels and actual levels is termed a 'controllable variance'. It is on the latter figure that you must concentrate if you want a realistic picture of how costs are performing.

If a full system of flexible budgetary control cannot be operated because of the difficulty of relating costs accurately to activity levels, you should consider introducing an updating system. This means that periodically during the year the budget is revised to meet changing conditions. This is sometimes called a rolling budget and, while it is not so effective as the fully flexible system, it is easier to operate.

Budgetary control

A budgetary control procedure is not easy to achieve. You have to work at it. There is no problem in designing a system with elegant forms and lots of information. The difficulty is in maintaining the scheme as a useful instrument once it has been set up. The impetus can only come from the top. The chief executive must insist on a rigorous approach to building budgets and a reporting procedure which is used to make things happen the way he wants them to happen. And he must ensure that everyone concerned knows what is expected of him and is accountable for any failure to perform.

Chapter 4
Case presentation

As a manager, you will frequently have to make out a case for what you think should be done. You have to persuade people to believe in your views and accept your recommendations. To do this, you must have a clear idea of what you want, and you have to show that you believe in it yourself. Above all, the effectiveness of your presentation will depend upon the care with which you have prepared it.

Preparation

Thorough preparation is vital. You must think through not only what should be done and why, but also how people will react. Only then can you decide how to make your case: stressing the benefits without underestimating the costs, and anticipating objections.

You should think of the questions your audience is likely to raise, and answer them in advance, or at least have your answers ready. The most likely questions are:

What — is the proposal?
 — will be the benefit?
 — will it cost?
 — are the facts, figures, forecasts and assumptions upon which the proposal is based?
 — are the alternatives?
Why — should we change what we are doing now?
 — is this proposal or solution better than the alternatives?
How — is the change to be made?
 — are the snags to be overcome?
 — have the alternatives been examined?
 — am I affected by the change?

Who — will be affected by the change and what will be their
     reaction?
    — is likely to have the strongest views for or against
     the change, and why?
    — will implement the proposal?
When — should this be done?

To make your case you have to do three things:

1. Show that it is based on a thorough analysis of the facts
   and that the alternatives were properly evaluated before
   the conclusion was reached. If you have made assumptions,
   you must demonstrate that these are reasonable on the
   basis of relevant experience and justifiable projections,
   which allow for the unexpected. Bear in mind Robert
   Heller's words that 'a proposal is only as strong as its
   weakest assumption'.
2. Spell out the benefits — to the company *and* the
   individuals to whom the case is being made. Wherever
   possible, express benefits in financial terms. Abstract
   benefits, such as customer satisfaction or workers' morale,
   are difficult to sell. But don't produce 'funny numbers' —
   financial justifications which will not stand up to
   examination.
3. Reveal costs. Don't try to disguise them in any way. And
   be realistic. Your proposition will be destroyed if anyone
   can show that you have underestimated the costs.

Remember, boards want to know in precise terms what they
will get for their money. Most boards are cautious, being
unwilling and often unable to take much risk. For this reason, it
is difficult to make a case for experiments or pilot schemes
unless the board, committee or individual can see what the real
benefits and the ultimate bill will be.

Presentation

Your proposal will often be made in two stages: a written
report followed by an oral presentation. The quality of the
latter will often tip the balance in your favour (or against you).
Making presentations and writing reports are dealt with in
Chapters 32 and 36 respectively, but it is appropriate to note at
this stage some special points you should bear in mind when
making a case orally in front of an audience:

1. Your presentation should not just consist of a repetition of the facts in the written report. It should be used to get across the main points of the argument, leaving out the detail.
2. Do not assume that your audience has read the written report or understood it. While you are talking, try to avoid referring to the report. This may switch people's attention from what you are saying. Use visual aids, preferably a flip chart, to emphasize the main points. But don't overdo them — it is possible to be too slick. The audience will be convinced by you, not by your elegant visual aids.
3. Make sure your opening secures people's attention. They must be immediately interested in your presentation. Begin by outlining your plan, its benefits and costs, and let the audience know how you are going to develop your case.
4. Bring out the disadvantages and the alternative courses of action so that you are not suspected of concealing or missing something.
5. Avoid being drawn into too much detail. Be succinct and to the point.
6. An emphatic summing up is imperative. It should convey with complete clarity what you want the board, committee or individual to do.

The effectiveness of your presentation will be largely dependent on how well you have prepared. Not only getting your facts, figures and arguments clearly down on paper but also deciding what you are going to say at the meeting and how you are going to say it. The more important the case the more carefully you should rehearse the presentation.

Checklist

1. Do you know exactly what you want?
2. Do you really believe in your case?
3. Have you obtained and checked all the facts that support your case?
4. What are the strongest arguments for your case?
5. Why must the present situation be changed?
6. Who else will be affected? Unions, other divisions or departments?
7. What are the arguments against your plan?
8. What alternatives are there to your plan?

9. To whom are you presenting your plan? Have you done any lobbying?
10. Have you discussed the finances with the experts?
11. Do you know who are your probable allies and who are likely to be your opponents?
12. Have you prepared handouts of any complicated figures?
13. Have you discussed the best time to present your case?
14. Your ideas were good when you first thought of them; are they still as good?

Chapter 5
Change management

Change is the only thing that remains constant in organizations. As A. P. Sloan said in *My Years with General Motors*: 'The circumstances of an ever-changing market and an ever-changing product are capable of breaking any business organization if that organization is unprepared for change.'

Change is inevitable. How, therefore, should you prepare for it and how should you manage it as it happens? To answer this question, you need to know something about:

☐ The process of change – the factors and forces that produce change
☐ Resistance to change – why and how people resist change
☐ How to overcome resistance to change.

The process of change

Change occurs in an organization because of internal and external factors. Changes in the environment which affect the enterprise are often unpredictable. You can try to predict their size and impact and prepare plans to meet them, but, for example, no model of the economy has yet been made that can reliably forecast the rate of inflation for more than 12 months ahead.

Internally, changes may take place in the company's product or service, the technology it uses, the people it employs, and its structure, which includes ownership as well as organization.

Internal and external factors interact in a complex manner. Corporate planners make lots of noise about analysing external threats and opportunities and internal strengths and weaknesses. But it all boils down to crystal ball gazing in the end. A wise man constantly expects the unexpected.

Organizations and the people in them would like to remain in equilibrium but cannot. Forces acting on them regularly create imbalances which disturb the pattern. This creates a demand for opposing forces to restore equilibrium.

Resistance to change

Resistance to change is natural. It arises because of:

Preference for stability
Human beings generally seek stability. The first reaction of most people affected by change is to try and regain their equilibrium.

Habit
Once a habit has been established it often provides comfort and satisfaction.

Conformity
Most people like to conform to the customary and expected ways of behaving; they are able to work together because each knows what to expect from the other. If anything diverging from the accepted norm is introduced into the environment it will be disruptive.

Threat to economic interests or prestige
This is perhaps the most obvious source of resistance. Joan Woodward made this point forcibly when she wrote:

> When we talk about resistance to change we tend to imply that this is an irrational behavioural tendency. There is a general assumption that management is always rational in changing its direction or modifying its objectives to achieve its goals better, and that operators are stupid, emotional or irrational in not responding in the way they should. But if an individual is going to be worse off explicitly or implicitly in any way when the proposed changes have been made, any resistance is entirely rational in terms of his own best interest. The interests of the organization and the individual do not always coincide.

People focus on their own best interests and often think that any change must be for the bad. Consider these two examples:

> The managing director of a rapidly growing organization decided that its size demanded the creation of a new product planning and development department to be headed by a director. This change would eliminate most of the decision-making power that the directors of marketing, engineering and production had over new

products. As new products were very important in this organization the change also reduced their much-valued status. During the two months after the managing director announced his idea for a new product director, the existing directors each came up with six or seven reasons why the new arrangement might not work. Their objections grew louder and louder until the managing director shelved the idea.

A manufacturing company had traditionally employed a large group of personnel people as counsellors and 'father confessors' to its production employees. Morale was high among these counsellors because of the professional satisfaction they received from the 'helping relationships' they had with employees. Then a new performance appraisal system was installed. Every six months the counsellors were required to provide each employee's supervisor with a written evaluation of the employee's 'emotional maturity', 'promotional potential' and so forth. The personnel people immediately recognized that the new system would alter their relationship to the employees from peer and helper to boss and evaluator. Predictably, they resisted the change. Arguing that the new system was not as good for the company as the old one, they put on as much pressure as possible until the new system was altered significantly.

Misunderstanding

People may not understand the implications of change and believe that it will cost them much more than they will gain. Such situations often occur when there is a lack of trust between the person initiating the change and the employees. Here is an example:

When the chairman of a small company announced to its managers that the company would implement a flexible working schedule for all employees, it never occurred to him that he might run into resistance. He had been introduced to the concept at a management course and decided to use it to make working conditions more attractive, particularly to clerical and factory personnel.

Shortly after the announcement numerous rumours began to circulate among factory employees, none of whom really knew what flexible working hours meant and many of whom were distrustful of the manufacturing manager. One rumour, for instance suggested that flexible hours meant that most people would have to work whenever their supervisors asked them to, including evenings and weekends. The union held a quick meeting and then presented the management with a non-negotiable demand that the flexible hours concept be dropped. The chairman, caught completely by surprise, complied.

Different perceptions

People may assess the situation differently from their managers or those initiating the change and see more costs than benefits resulting from the change, not only for themselves but for their company as well. For example:

> The president of one moderate size US bank was shocked by his staff's analysis of the bank's real estate investment trust (REIT) loans. This complicated analysis suggested that the bank could easily lose up to $10 million, and the possible losses were increasing each month by 10 per cent. Within a week, the president drew up a plan to reorganize the part of the bank that managed REITs. Because of his concern for the bank's stock price, however, he chose not to release the staff report to anyone except the new REIT section manager.
>
> The reorganization immediately ran into massive resistance from the people involved. The group sentiment as articulated by one person, was: 'Has he gone mad? Why in God's name is he tearing apart this section of the bank? His actions have already cost us three very good people (who quit) and have crippled a new programme we were implementing (which the president was unaware of) to reduce our loan losses.'

Overcoming resistance to change

While people often take an antagonistic or negative attitude to change, it is also true that the desire for new experience underlies much of human behaviour. This fact will help you overcome resistance to change. People come to accept change in three ways:

☐ *Compliance*, or 'do it because I say so'. The individual accepts the change because he has to. He does not necessarily believe in what he has to do.

☐ *Identification*, or 'do it because I do it'. The individual defines his own beliefs and actions in terms of what someone else is or does. Identification is like compliance in that the individual does not agree to change because it is satisfying. It differs from compliance, however, in that the individual actually believes in the opinions and actions he adopts.

☐ *Intrinsic satisfaction*, or 'do it because it is worth doing'. The individual accepts change because the new situation is intrinsically satisfying or because it is in accordance with his own set of values. He may be influenced by others in forming this view, but ultimately he accepts the change because he likes it rather than because someone else likes it.

Resistance to change will be less if:

- [ ] Those affected by change feel that they can accept the project as their own, not one imposed upon them by outsiders
- [ ] The change has the wholehearted support of management
- [ ] The change accords with well-established values
- [ ] The change is seen as reducing rather than increasing present burdens
- [ ] The change offers the kind of new experience which interests participants
- [ ] Participants feel that their autonomy and security are not threatened
- [ ] Participants have jointly diagnosed the problems
- [ ] The change has been agreed by group decisions
- [ ] Those advocating change understand the feelings and fears of those affected and take steps to relieve unnecessary fears
- [ ] It is recognized that new ideas are likely to be misinterpreted and ample provision is made for discussion of reactions to proposals to ensure complete understanding of them.

A case study

A customer service department had a large section of about 40 people — mainly women — who dealt with correspondence. A large proportion of the letters contained complaints from customers about how their accounts had been handled.

Unfortunately, the data required to answer letters were not immediately accessible. Some data were held in the computer while the rest were contained in individual customer files which were often split between different locations or products. Consequently, there were delays in answering letters and, because the full picture was not readily available, some replies did not answer the complaint specifically enough and generated additional complaints.

The female clerks in the department had been working this system for a number of years and had got used to it. Staff turnover was very low (less than 10 per cent per year) and there was no pressure from them for any change.

Management, however, wanted to improve the accuracy of replies and speed up their processing. A new computer-linked system could be developed which would achieve both these aims *and* save staff. The work would be no more demanding and could even bring greater job satisfaction because of the facility for dealing comprehensively and quickly with individual customers without leaving any loose ends.

A carefully planned programme of change management was therefore worked out. Preliminary informal meetings were held with small groups of staff to sound out their feelings about the present system and how they would like it to be improved. They were told that there were a number of possible ways of doing this but that no plans would be finalized until their ideas had been taken into account.

When the initial ideas of management were presented to the staff the benefits to the individual were emphasized — less hassle, not so much effort spent in walking about the building getting information, and the satisfaction they could gain from being given greater responsibility. They were not bribed with more money nor was the fact that there would be some staff savings disguised. But it was emphasized that any staff surplus would be taken up by natural wastage. The staff were also told that the scheme would be tested thoroughly using a small team of volunteers who would be consulted continuously about their work. Progress reports to all the staff of the department would also be issued regularly.

The staff accepted this proposal because they recognized that the company clearly stood to gain by the new system, and they themselves would not lose and might even benefit in a number of ways. The pilot test was carried out, consultation took place as planned, and the full scheme was implemented on time and without any fuss.

Chapter 6

Clear thinking

...ess of reasoning by
...other and correct
... Clear thinking is
... what is relevant,

...n that he draws reason-
...be proved by reference to
the facts used to support them. He avoids ill-founded and
tendentious arguments, generalizations and irrelevancies. His
chain of reasoning is clear, unemotional and based on relevant
facts.

Clear thinking — a logical approach to problem-solving,
decision-making and case presentation — is an essential attribute
of an effective manager. This does not mean that it is the only
way to think. Edward de Bono has made out an incontrovertible
case for lateral, ie creative, thinking as a necessary process for
innovative managers to use alongside the more traditional
vertical or logical thinking pattern (see Chapter 12). But a
logical approach is still an essential requirement.

A further attribute of a good manager is the ability to argue
persuasively and to detect the flaws in other people's arguments.
To think clearly and to argue well, you need to understand first,
how to develop a proposition or a case from basic principles;
second, how to test your proposition; and third, how to avoid
using fallacious arguments and how to expose the fallacies used
by others.

Developing a proposition

The first rule of the old Training Within Industry programme
for supervisors was 'get the facts'. It is still the starting point for
clear thinking. The facts must be relevant to the issue under

consideration. If comparisons are being made, like must be compared with like. Trends must be related to an appropriate base date and, if trends are being compared, the same base should be used. Treat opinions with caution until they are supported by evidence. Avoid a superficial analysis of surface data. Dig deep. Take nothing for granted. Sift the evidence and discard what is irrelevant.

Your inferences should be derived *directly* from the facts. Where possible, the connection between the facts and the conclusion should be shown to be justified on the basis of verifiable and relevant experience or information on similar relationships occurring elsewhere.

If, as is likely, more than one inference can be deduced from the facts, you should test each inference to establish which one most clearly derives from the evidence as supported by experience. But it is no good saying 'it stands to reason' or 'it's common sense'. You have to produce the evidence which proves that the inference is reasonable and you have to pin down the vague concept of common sense to the data and experience upon which it is based. It was Descartes who wrote: 'Common sense is the best distributed commodity in the world, for every man is convinced that he is well supplied with it.'

Testing propositions

Susan Stebbing wrote: 'We are content to accept without testing any belief that fits in with our prejudices and whose truth is necessary for the satisfaction of our desires.' Clear thinking must try to avoid this trap.

When we form a proposition or belief we generalize from what is observed — our own analysis or experience — and thence infer to what is not observed. We also refer to testimony — other people's observations and experience.

If your proposition or belief is derived from a generalization based upon particular instances you should test it by answering the following questions:

☐ Was the scope of the investigation sufficiently comprehensive?
☐ Are the instances representative or are they selected to support a point of view?
☐ Are there contradictory instances that have not been looked for?

☐ Does the proposition or belief in question conflict with other beliefs for which we have equally good grounds?

☐ If there are any conflicting beliefs or contradictory items of evidence have they been put to the test against the original proposition?

☐ Could the evidence or testimony lead to other equally valid conclusions?

☐ Are there any other factors which have not been taken into account which may have influenced the evidence and, therefore, the conclusion?

If your belief is based on testimony, you should test the reliability of the testimony, its relevance to the point, and whether or not your belief follows logically from the evidence, ie can reasonably be inferred from the facts.

Fallacious and misleading arguments

A fallacy is an unsound form of argument leading to a mistake in reasoning or a misleading impression. The main fallacies to avoid or to spot in other people's arguments are:

☐ Sweeping statements
☐ Potted thinking
☐ Special pleading
☐ Over-simplification
☐ Reaching false conclusions
☐ Begging the question
☐ False analogy
☐ Using words ambiguously
☐ Chop logic.

These are discussed briefly below.

Sweeping statements
In our desire for certainty and to carry the point we often indulge in sweeping statements. We sometimes then repeat them more and more loudly and angrily in order to convince our opponent. If we do it often enough and forcibly enough we can even deceive ourselves.

It has been said that 'it's never fair, it's never wise, it's never safe to generalize'. But that is a generalization in itself. Scientific method is based on generalizations. They can be valid if they are inferred properly from adequate, relevant and reliable evidence.

Generalizations are invalid when they have been produced by over-simplifying the facts or by selecting instances favourable to a contention while ignoring those that conflict with it. The classic form of a fallacious generalization is the contention that if some A is B then all A must be B. What frequently happens is that people say A is B when all they know is that *some* A is B or, at most A *tends* to be B. The argument is misleading unless the word 'some' or 'tends' is admitted.

Many of the fallacies considered below are special cases of unsafe generalization, the most common symptom of unsound reasoning.

Potted thinking

Potted thinking happens when we argue using slogans and catch phrases, when we extend an assertion in an unwarrantable fashion.

It is natural to form confident beliefs about complicated matters when we are proposing or taking action. And it is equally natural to compress these beliefs into a single phrase or thought. But it is dangerous to accept compressed statements that save us the trouble of thinking. They are only acceptable if fresh thinking has preceded them.

Special pleading

If anyone says to you: 'everyone knows that', 'it's obvious that' or 'it's indisputably true that', you can be certain that he has taken for granted what he is about to assert.

We indulge in special pleading when we stress our own case and fail to see that there may be other points of view, other ways of looking at the question. Special pleading happens when we cannot detach ourselves from our own circumstances. We often blunder because we forget that what is true of one of us is also true of the other in the same situation.

A safeguard against this mistake is to change *you* into *I*. Thus, *I* feel that you can't see what is straight in front of your nose; *you* feel that I can't see what is on the other side of my blinkers. A rule that appears to be sound when I apply it to you may seem to be unsatisfactory when you ask me to apply it to myself.

Of course, thinking for too long about other points of view is a recipe for indecision. There are not necessarily two sides to every question and even if there are, you eventually — and often quickly — have to come down firmly on one side. But before you do this, check in case the other points of view or the alternative approaches are valid, and take them into account.

Over-simplification

Over-simplification is a special form of potted thinking or special pleading. It often arises in the form of what Susan Stebbing terms 'the fallacy of either black or white', the mistake of demanding that a sharp line should be drawn, when in fact no sharp line can be drawn. For example, we cannot ask for a clear distinction to be drawn between the sane and the insane, or between the intelligent and the unintelligent. Our readiness to make this mistake may be taken advantage of by a dishonest opponent, who insists that we define precisely that which does not admit of such definition.

Reaching false conclusions

One of the most prevalent fallacies is that of forming the view that because *some* are or may be, *all* are. An assertion about several cases is twisted into an assertion about all cases. The conclusion does not follow the premise.

The most common form of this fallacy is what logicians call the 'undistributed middle', which refers to the traditional syllogism consisting of a premise, a middle term and a conclusion.

A valid syllogism takes the following form:

Premise : All cows are quadrupeds.
Middle term : All quadrupeds are vertebrates.
Conclusion : Therefore, all cows are vertebrates.

This may be represented as:

Premise : All A is B.
Middle term : All B is C.
Conclusion : Therefore, all A is C.

This is logical. The middle term is fully distributed. Everything that applies to A, also applies to B, everything that applies to B also applies to C, therefore, everything that applies to A must apply to C.

An invalid syllogism would take the following form:

All cows are quadrupeds.
All mules are quadrupeds.
Therefore, all mules are cows.

This may be represented as:

> All A is B.
> All C is B.
> Therefore, all A is C.

This is false because, although everything that applies to A and C also applies to B, there is nothing in their relationship to B which connects A and C together.

The difference between the true and false syllogism may be illustrated as follows.

True Syllogism   *False Syllogism*

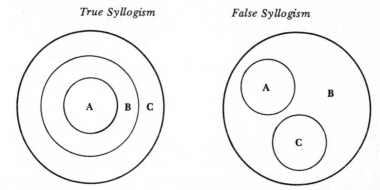

In the false syllogism, A and C could be quite distinct although still contained within B. To link them together goes beyond the original evidence. Because two things A and B are related to another thing, C, it does not *necessarily* mean that they are related together. In forming arguments, we too often jump to the conclusion that *some* means *all*.

Allowing the conclusion to go beyond the evidence can also take the form of assuming that because we are aware of the effect (the *consequent*), we also know the cause (the *antecedent*). But this assumption may be incorrect. An effect can have many different causes. This fallacy of the consequent, as it is termed, can be illustrated by the following example:

> If he came up on the pools, he would go to the West Indies.
> He has gone to the West Indies.
> Therefore he has come up on the pools.

> ie If P then Q,
> Q
> Therefore P.

But there are a number of other reasons why he could have gone to the West Indies besides coming up on the pools. A clear inference can only be drawn if the cause is directly related to the effect, thus:

> If he comes up on the pools he will go to the West Indies.
> He has come up on the pools.
> Therefore he will go to the West Indies.

> ie If P then Q,
>   P
>   Therefore Q.

A further danger in drawing conclusions from evidence is to forget that circumstances may alter cases. What has happened in the past will not necessarily happen again unless the circumstances are the same. You may be able to infer something from history but you cannot rely on that inference. Times change.

Begging the question
We beg the question when we take for granted what has yet to be proved. This can take the form of assuming the point in dispute without adequate reason; what the logicians call *petitio principio*.

If you spot someone taking for granted a premise which is not contained in his conclusion you must challenge the assumption and ask for information about the premises upon which the conclusion is based. You can then assess whether or not the conclusion follows logically from those premises.

Challenging assumptions is a necessary part of thinking clearly. You should challenge your own assumptions as well as those made by others.

False analogy
Analogy forms the basis of much of our thinking. We notice that two cases resemble each other in certain respects and then infer an extension of the resemblance. Analogies also aid understanding of an unfamiliar topic.

Analogies can be used falsely as vivid arguments without any real evidence. Just because A is B where both are familiar matters of fact, does not mean that X is Y, where X and Y are unfamiliar or abstract. When we argue by analogy we claim that if:

x has properties of p1, p2, p3 and f, and
y has properties of p1, p2 and p3, therefore
y also has the property of f.

This could be true unless y has a property incompatible with f, in which case the argument is unsound.

Analogies may be used to suggest a conclusion but they cannot establish it. They can be carried too far. Sometimes their relevance is more apparent than real.

Use argument by analogy to help support a case but do not rely upon it. Don't allow anyone else to get away with far-fetched analogies. They should be tested and their relevance should be proved.

Using words ambiguously

The Lewis Carroll approach — 'When I use a word it means just what I choose it to mean, neither more nor less' — is a favourite trick of those who aim to deceive. People use words that beg the question, that is, they define a word in a special way that supports their argument. They shift the meaning of words in different contexts. They may choose words which have the same meaning as each other but which show approval or disapproval. There is a well known saying that the word 'firm' can be declined as follows: 'I am firm, You are obstinate, He is pigheaded.'

Chop logic

'Contrariwise,' continued Tweedledee, 'if it was so, it might be, and if it were so, it would be; but as it isn't, it ain't. That's logic.'

Chop logic is not quite as bad as that, but it can be equally misleading. It includes such debating tricks as:

☐ Selecting instances favourable to a contention while ignoring those that conflict with it
☐ Twisting an argument advanced by an opponent to mean something quite different from what was intended — putting words in someone's mouth
☐ Diverting an opponent by throwing on him the burden of proving something he has not maintained
☐ Deliberately ignoring the point in dispute
☐ Introducing irrelevant matter into the argument
☐ Reiterating what has been denied and ignoring what has been asserted.

Chapter 7
Communicating

People recognize the need to communicate but find it difficult.
Like Schopenhauer's hedgehogs, they want to get together, it's
only their prickles that keep them apart.

Words may sound or look precise, but they are not. All sorts
of barriers exist between the communicator and the receiver.
Unless these barriers are overcome the message will be distorted
or will not get through.

Barriers to communication

Hearing what we want to hear
What we hear or understand when someone speaks to us is
largely based on our own experience and background. Instead
of hearing what people have told us, we hear what our minds
tell us they have said. We have preconceptions about what
people are going to say, and if what they say does not fit into
our framework of reference we adjust it until it does.

Ignoring conflicting information
We tend to ignore or reject communications that conflict with
our own beliefs. If they are not rejected, some way is found of
twisting and shaping their meaning to fit our preconceptions.
When a message is inconsistent with existing beliefs, the receiver
rejects its validity, avoids further exposure to it, easily forgets
it and, in his memory, distorts what he has heard.

Perceptions about the communicator
It is difficult to separate what we hear from our feelings about
the person who says it. Non-existent motives may be ascribed to
the communicator. If we like someone we are more likely to
accept what he says — whether it is right or wrong — than if we
dislike him.

46

Influence of the group
The group with which we identify influences our attitudes and feelings. What a group hears depends on its interests. Workers are more likely to listen to their colleagues, who share their experiences, than to outsiders such as managers or union officials.

Words mean different things to different people
Essentially, language is a method of using symbols to represent facts and feelings. Strictly speaking, we can't convey *meaning*; all we can do is to convey *words*. Do not assume that because something has a certain meaning to you, it will convey the same meaning to someone else.

Non-verbal communication
When we try to understand the meaning of what people say we listen to the words but we use other clues which convey meaning. We attend not only to *what* people say but to *how* they say it. We form impressions from what is called 'body language' — eyes, shape of the mouth, the muscles of the face, even posture. We may feel that these tell us more about what someone is really saying than the words he uses. But there is enormous scope for misinterpretation.

Emotions
Our emotions colour our ability to convey or to receive the true message. When we are insecure or worried, what we hear seems more threatening than when we are secure and at peace with the world. When we are angry or depressed, we tend to reject what might otherwise seem like reasonable requests or good ideas. During heated argument, many things said may not be understood or may be badly distorted.

Noise
Any interference to communication is 'noise'. It can be literal noise which prevents the message being heard, or figurative in the shape of distracting or confused information which distorts or obscures the meaning.

Size
The larger and more complex the organization, the greater the problem of communication. The more levels of management and supervision through which a message has to pass, the greater

the opportunity for distortion or misunderstanding.

Overcoming barriers to communication

Adjust to the world of the receiver
Try to predict the impact of what you are going to write or say on the receiver's feelings and attitudes. Tailor the message to fit the receiver's vocabulary, interests and values. Be aware of how the information might be misinterpreted because of prejudices, the influence of others and the tendency of people to reject what they do not want to hear.

Use feedback
Ensure that you get a message back from the receiver which tells you how much has been understood.

Use face-to-face communication
Whenever possible talk to people rather than write to them. That is how you get feedback. You can adjust or change your message according to reactions. You can also deliver it in a more human and understanding way — this can help to overcome prejudices. Verbal criticism can often be given in a more constructive manner than written reproof which always seems to be harsher.

Use reinforcement
You may have to present your message in a number of different ways to get it across. Re-emphasize the important points and follow up.

Use direct simple language
This seems obvious. But many people clutter up what they say with jargon, long words and elaborate sentences.

Suit the actions to the word
Communications have to be credible to be effective. When you say you are going to do something, do it. Next time you are more likely to be believed.

Use different channels
Some communications have to be in writing to get the message across promptly and without any variations in the way they

are delivered. But, wherever possible, supplement written communications with the spoken word. Conversely, an oral briefing should be reinforced in writing.

Reduce problems of size
If you can, reduce the number of levels of management. Encourage a reasonable degree of informality in communications. Ensure that activities are grouped together to ease communication on matters of mutual concern.

Chapter 8
Conflict management

You will not escape conflict in your organization. It is inevitable, because the objectives, values and needs of groups and individuals in the organization do not always coincide.

Conflict may be a sign of a healthy organization. Bland agreement on everything would be unnatural and enervating. There should be clashes of ideas about tasks and projects, and disagreements should not be suppressed. They should come out into the open, because that is the only way in which you can ensure that the issues are explored and conflicts are resolved. There is such a thing as creative conflict. But conflict becomes counter-productive when it is based on personality clashes, or when it is treated as an unseemly mess to be hurriedly cleared away, rather than as a problem to be 'worked -through'.

Resolving conflict

There are three principal ways of resolving conflict.

Peaceful co-existence
The aim here is to smooth out differences and emphasize the common ground. People are encouraged to learn to live together; there is a good deal of information, contact and exchange of views, and individuals move freely between groups (eg between headquarters and the field, or between sales and manufacturing).

This is a pleasant ideal, but it may not be practicable in many situations. There is much evidence that conflict is not necessarily resolved by grouping people together. Improved communications and techniques such as briefing groups may appear to be good ideas but are useless if management has nothing to say that people want to hear. There is also the danger that the real issues, submerged for the moment in an atmosphere of superficial bonhomie, will surface again at a later date.

Compromise
The issue is resolved by negotiation or bargaining and neither party wins or loses. This concept of splitting the difference is essentially pessimistic. The hallmark of this approach is that there is no 'right' or 'best' answer. Agreements only accommodate differences. Real issues are not likely to be solved.

Problem solving
An attempt is made to find a genuine solution to the problem rather than just accommodating different points of view. This is where the apparent paradox of 'creative conflict' comes in. Conflict situations can be used to advantage to create better solutions.

If solutions are to be developed by problem solving, they have to be generated by those who share the responsibility for seeing that the solutions work. The sequence of actions is: first, those concerned work to define the problem and agree on the objectives to be attained in reaching a solution; second, the group develops alternative solutions and debates their merits; third, agreement is reached on the preferred course of action and how it should be implemented.

Conflict, as has been said, is in itself not to be deplored; it is an inevitable concomitant of progress and change. What is to be deplored is the failure to use conflict constructively. Effective problem solving both resolves conflicts and opens up channels of discussion and cooperative action.

Over 50 years ago one of the pioneering writers on management, Mary Parker Follett, wrote something on managing conflict which is as valid today as it was then: 'Differences can be made to contribute to the common cause if they are resolved by integration rather than domination or compromise.'

Case studies

Who should do market research?
A new market research manager had been engaged. Described by her boss as 'pushy' she quite naturally wanted to establish her position quickly.

Her predecessor had been a quiet fellow who had come to an

arrangement with the head of operational research that they should divide the market research activity between them: external field research was conducted by the market research manager and internal research on customer buying habits was conducted within the operational research department.

The new market research manager would have none of this. She believed that her department should handle all research and analysis concerning customer behaviour. Any division would be artificial. The operational research manager strongly disagreed. He could advance the rational argument that the information wanted for internal research was on the computer to which he had immediate access and the skills and resources to use. In any case, he liked to feel that he and his department were in touch with current issues and were not just operating in a small back room divorced from reality.

Both those involved felt equally strongly that they were right. Their divisional head tried to get them to accept a compromise solution which would make the operational research manager responsible for the initial collection and analysis of the internal data while the market research manager would collate and comment on the information for the benefit of the marketing department.

Having failed to impose this compromise, the divisional head called on the help of a management consultant friend of his who specialized in dealing with this sort of situation. The consultant saw each of the parties separately to get a full run-down of facts and opinions. He then persuaded them to sit down together, with the divisional head, and, by the end of the day, to try to come up with an integrated solution about which everyone would be happy — no compromises. The consultant emphasized that the aim was to come up with a solution that would not leave either party with the feeling that they had lost something.

The original discussions which the consultant held with each of the managers helped them to leave their emotions outside the meeting and to concentrate on coming up with a mutually acceptable solution. And, eventually, this is what they did. Each agreed to collect external and internal data separately from their respective sources. They would then jointly analyse and present their findings to marketing management. This solution was implemented and it worked. The rivalry between them largely vanished and a better service was provided to marketing.

The canteen crisis

The union was most unhappy about the decision to increase canteen prices by the amount of inflation without any prior consultation. The new factory manager said that it was generally understood that prices, like wages, had to keep pace with inflation and that there was nothing in the procedural agreement which stated that consultation was necessary before increasing prices.

The union convenor admitted that the agreement contained no specific reference to canteen prices but pointed out that terms and conditions of employment were negotiable and asked: 'If canteen prices aren't terms and conditions of employment, what are they?'

The factory manager, however, would not budge and the union called for a ban on overtime and a work-to-rule which was particularly damaging at that time.

The divisional personnel director was despatched urgently to the factory to sort things out. He wanted to achieve a settlement in which neither side would have to give in completely to the other but which, without compromise, would satisfy all parties. His approach was to call for a joint 'problem-solving' meeting of union and management. There were to be no recriminations, only an analysis of how to get out of the impasse and how to set up an arrangement which would prevent it happening again.

The meeting started by being rowdy, but the personnel director rapidly de-fused it by insisting that they were there to discuss and solve a problem, not to shout at one another. He provided the union with a full analysis of the canteen accounts and an explanation why price increases were necessary. He agreed to modify the increases where the union showed that the charges were not absolutely justified. And, most important, he got agreement to a joint arrangement for monitoring the canteen accounts and agreeing on any price increases required before announcements were made. Management got most of the increases they wanted, normal working was resumed and the union felt it was in a stronger position than before. Honour was satisfied on all sides.

Chapter 9

Controlling

Basically, you are seeking to control two things — input and output — and the relationship between them, which is productivity or performance. All managers will know Murphy's two laws: if anything can go wrong, it will; and of the things that can't go wrong, some will.

The aim of good control is to protect your plans from the operation of these laws as far as possible. To detect trouble spots before they erupt. To prevent those accidents which are just waiting to happen. Prevention is better than cure.

Essentials of control

Control is relative. It does not deal with absolutes, only with the difference between good and not-so-good performance.

The basis of control is measurement. It depends on accurate information about what is being achieved. This is then compared with what *should* have been achieved and with what has been achieved in the past. But that is only a starting point. Good control also identifies responsibility and points the way to action.

Effective control
If you want to exercise good control you need to:

1. *Plan* what you aim to achieve
2. *Measure* regularly what has been achieved
3. *Compare* actual achievements with the plan
4. *Take action* to exploit opportunities revealed by this information or to correct deviations from the plan.

Note that control is not only a matter of putting things right. It also has a positive side — getting more or better things done on the basis of information received.

Problems of control

A good control system is not easy to set up. There are two essentials:

☐ To set appropriate and fair targets, standards and budgets. (This may be difficult where the scope for quantification is limited or if circumstances make forecasts unreliable.)

☐ To decide what information is crucial for control purposes and design reports which clearly convey that information to the people who need it and can use it to point the way to action. This also produces problems. Too many control systems generate a surfeit of indigestible data which go to the wrong people and are not acted upon. You can have too little information, but there is also such a thing as information overkill. There is, moreover, a tendency for some people to report good results and cover up poor results. In any case, the figures may not tell the whole story.

Overcoming the problem

There are five steps to take if you want to achieve good control:

1. Decide what you want to control
2. Decide how you are going to measure and review performance
3. Use ratio analysis to make comparisons and to identify variations and problems
4. Set up a control system
5. Manage by exception.

Controlling inputs and outputs

In controlling input and output, and hence productivity, an overview is essential. It is no good concentrating on inputs, mainly expressed as costs, unless you look at the benefits arising from these expenditures and the effectiveness with which the costs have been incurred. Cost benefit and cost effectiveness studies are an essential part of the control process.

Input control

When you control inputs you should aim to measure and assess the performance of:

☐ *Money* — its productivity, flow, liquidity and conservation. You need to know what return you are getting on investments compared with the return you want.

You should ensure that you have the cash and working capital to run the business. Cash flow analysis is vital. One of the golden rules of management as stated by Robert Heller, is 'cash in must exceed cash out'.

You must conserve and provide the money needed to finance future trading and development projects and for capital investment.

Management has to know how effectively its financial resources are being used to produce goods, services and profits and this requires continuous and close attention to the control of direct and indirect costs and overheads generally.

☐ *People* — the effectiveness of the people you employ in terms of their quality and performance

☐ *Materials* — their availability, condition, convertibility and waste

☐ *Equipment* — machine utilization and capability.

Output control

☐ *Quantitative control measures* — the units produced or sold, the amount of services provided, the sales turnover obtained and the profits achieved. Key performance measures will vary between organizations. You need to determine through analysis which are the crucial indicators of success or failure.

☐ *Qualitative control measures* — the level of service provided by an organization (eg a public corporation) or by a non-productive department within an organization (eg personnel). It is more difficult to select valid performance measures in these areas, but the attempt should be made.

Productivity control

Productivity is the relationship between input and output. Cost benefit studies are productivity studies in that they assess how much benefit (output) is obtained from a given cost (input).

Productivity is expressed by ratios. A productivity index can be produced as follows:

$$\text{productivity index} = \frac{\text{output}}{\text{input}} = \frac{\text{performance achieved}}{\text{resources consumed}} = \frac{\text{effectiveness}}{\text{efficiency}}$$

Ratio analysis

Expressing items as percentages or ratios of other items — ratio analysis — is the best way to measure and control inputs, outputs, productivity and the financial resources of the company generally. Ratios should not, however, be used in isolation. You should always take account of trends between present and past performance. And you should compare ratios within the business and between your business and other businesses. Most importantly, you should compare actual ratios with planned ratios.

It is essential to seek the *key* indicators in the form of ratios, for your business. You will not want to collect sheets of ratios from every direction, but you should know when you look at a set of figures which one you have got to divide into the other to tell you what is really happening. It is no good just knowing how much sales have increased over the last period. You also need to know how the number of sales representatives has changed and the volume of sales per representative, this period compared with budget, the last period, and the same period last year.

The most important financial and productivity ratios are described below.

Return on capital employed
This is usually expressed as net profit as a percentage of capital. It tells you the extent to which an investment is paying off. It could apply to the whole business from the point of view of the shareholders; to part of the business, or to the specific return on an investment in capital equipment. When compared with the return you could get if you invested your money elsewhere, this ratio indicates the extent to which the investment is justified.

This can lead into an analysis of opportunity costs which are the costs as compared with the profit or loss expected from an alternative investment or course of action. In other words, if you failed to make a decision or take an opportunity that would have produced a better result than the decision you did make, that lost revenue is an 'opportunity cost'.

When analysing returns on capital employed, be careful to check the basis of the figures to ensure that like is compared with like. A common, but not universal, definition of capital employed includes share capital, reserves (excluding those for taxation), long-term loans and bank overdraft. The return figure is usually defined as net profit, excluding tax and interest on capital.

Tax is excluded because its varying nature makes it difficult to compare data from year to year. Interest on capital is omitted because its inclusion would mean that the return on capital would be measured *after* a return had been obtained on investment. Bear in mind that comparisons can be distorted when there are few fixed assets, for example when plant is rented or leased by the company.

Profit to sales ratio

This is the fundamental measure of the profitability of the company as a trading concern. It is expressed as a ratio:

$$\frac{\text{Net trading profit (ie the difference between expenses and income from sales)}}{\text{Sales revenue}}$$

Solvency ratios

These measure the company's short-term financial liabilities — its ability to pay its current liabilities as they fall due.

The 'current' ratio is calculated as follows:

$$\frac{\text{Current assets (stock, debtors and cash)}}{\text{Current liabilities (creditors and accrued charges)}}$$

If the current ratio is more than 1:1, then the company has more current assets than current liabilities and, if it were forced to pay out all its current liabilities, would have sufficient current assets to do so.

If a really strict appraisal of a company's solvency is required, however, it is best to leave stock out of the current assets, and to take only the liquid assets into consideration. This is because if a company were forced to realize its stock quickly, it is doubtful if it would even recover its cost value. The ratio then becomes:

$$\frac{\text{Current assets excluding stock}}{\text{Current liabilities}}$$

This is sometimes called the 'acid test'. Ideally the ratio should be at least 1:1 but there are cases where a ratio of somewhat less than 1:1 is acceptable. Too high a ratio, on the other hand, would mean that the company is not making sufficient use of its finances — cash by itself does not generate much profit.

Stock ratios

If the company holds too much stock it will be wasting its financial resources in an unused asset. If it holds too little stock it will lose sales revenue through not being able to service its customers.

To measure how much is being tied up in stock use the ratio:

$$\frac{\text{Stock}}{\text{Current assets}}$$

To measure how quickly the stock is turned over (stock turn) the ratio is:

$$\frac{\text{Sales}}{\text{Stock}}$$

The greater the stock turnover figure the better for the company. If the goods are being sold at a profit, then the more that are sold the better the profit at the year end.

Other financial ratios

There are a number of other financial ratios you can use. Perhaps the most important are:

$$\frac{\text{Debtors}}{\text{Average daily sales}}$$

This measures how well management is speeding the flow of cash through the business, ie how many days' credit is being allowed to customers.

$$\frac{\text{Debtors}}{\text{Creditors}}$$

If creditors begin to outweigh debtors this may be a sign that the company is over-trading. The bad debt ratio (bad debts/sales) is also revealing.

$$\frac{\text{Current liabilities} - (\text{current assets minus stock})}{\text{Profit before tax and interest} } \times 365$$

This is the current liquidity ratio. It shows how many days it would take at current profit levels to pay off the deficit between current liabilities and liquid assets.

Productivity ratios

The most useful productivity ratio is:

$$\frac{\text{results}}{\text{resources}} \quad \text{ie} \quad \frac{\text{sales}}{\text{employees}}$$

The other main ratios are:

$$\frac{\text{units produced or processed}}{\text{number of employees}}$$

$$\frac{\text{added value (ie sales revenue minus cost of sales)}}{\text{number of employees}}$$

$$\frac{\text{profit after tax}}{\text{number of employees}}$$

Cost ratios

The best way to look at costs is to express them as a percentage of sales. Thus the fundamental measure is:

$$\frac{\text{overheads}}{\text{sales}} \times 100$$

Other measures include:

$$\frac{\text{payroll costs}}{\text{sales}} \times 100$$

$$\frac{\text{cost of materials and bought in parts}}{\text{sales}} \times 100$$

$$\frac{\text{selling costs}}{\text{sales}} \times 100$$

Use of ratios

Use ratios as you would use any other figures. They are no more than indicators. In themselves, they will not tell the whole story. You have to dig. A ratio is no more than a symptom. You need to find out the real cause of a variation or problem.

Control systems

What you need from a control system

Your basic requirement is reports that clearly identify areas of good and bad performance so that appropriate action can be taken.

At higher levels 'exception reporting' should be adopted so that significant deviations, on which action should be taken, can be highlighted. Overall summaries of performance against plan and of trends will also be necessary at this level, but these may disguise significant underlying deviations which would be pointed out in an exception report.

The reports themselves should:

- [ ] Contain measurements which are accurate, valid and reliable. Permit a direct and easy comparison between planned and actual performance
- [ ] Analyse trends, comparing one period's performance with that of the previous period or of the same period the previous year and, where appropriate, summarizing the year to date position
- [ ] Be given to the person who is responsible for the activity concerned
- [ ] Arrive promptly, in time to allow the necessary action to be taken
- [ ] Provide succinct explanations of any deviations from plan.

Measurements

Measurement is a good thing, but all figures need to be treated with caution. They may conceal more than they reveal. The weaknesses to look for are:

- [ ] *Non-representative reporting* — data selected which do not cover the key issues, disguise unfavourable results or over-emphasize favourable performance.
- [ ] *Not comparing like with like* — the 'apples and pears syndrome'. For example, a trend or projection which does not take account of changing or new factors which have altered or will alter the situation since the base data were collected.
- [ ] *Not starting from a common base.* This is a variant on the 'like with like' problem. Trend comparisons should be related to a common base in terms both of the period and the elements covered by the information.
- [ ] *Misleading averages.* Averages do not always tell you the whole story. They may conceal extremes in performance, which are significant.
- [ ] *Unintentional errors* — simple mistakes in calculation, presentation or observation.
- [ ] *Measurements out of context.* Almost any single measure is influenced by, or inseparable from, other measures. Figures in isolation may not mean very much. You have to know about relationships and underlying influences.

Management by exception

Management by exception is a system which rings alarm bells

only when the manager's attention is needed. The principle was invented by the father of scientific management, Frederick Taylor. In 1911 he wrote:

> Under the exception principle the manager should receive only condensed, summarized and invariably comparative reports covering, however, all of the elements entering into the management and even these summaries should all be carefully gone over by an assistant before they reach the manager, and have all the exceptions to the past averages or standards pointed out, both the especially good and the especially bad exceptions, thus giving him in a few minutes a full view of progress which is being made, or the reverse, and leaving him free to consider the broader lines of policy and to study the character and fitness of the important men under him.

Management by exception frees the boss to concentrate on the things that matter. It gives the subordinate more scope to get on with his work while knowing that events out of the ordinary will be reported upwards.

Deciding what constitutes an exception is a useful exercise in itself. It means selecting the key events and measures which will show up good, bad or indifferent results and indicate whether or not performance is going according to plan.

The chosen indicators or ratios can be studied so that the significance of changes or trends is readily understood. More importantly, the possible causes of deviations can be analysed and kept in mind. Investigations will then be quickly launched in the right direction and swift remedial action can be taken.

Most of us have come across the boss or manager who seems to have the almost magic facility for studying a mass of figures and immediately spotting the one really important deviation or the item that does not ring true. It sometimes seems to be pure instinct, but of course it is not. Such managers are practising the art of management by exception, even if they never call it by that name. Their experience and analytical powers have told them what constitutes normal performance. But they can spot something out of the ordinary at a thousand paces. They *know* what the key indicators are and they look for them, hard. This is a skill that anyone can develop. And the effort of acquiring it is well worthwhile.

Chapter 10
Coordinating

Coordinating — 'achieving unity of effort', in Urwick's phrase — is not a separate function of a manager. As Sune Carlson wrote: 'The concept of coordination does not describe a *particular* set of operations but *all* operations which lead to a certain result.'

Coordination is required because individual actions need to be synchronized. Some activities must follow one another in sequence. Others must go on at the same time and in the same direction in order to finish together.

How to coordinate

Obviously, you can get good coordination if you get people to work well together. This means integrating their activities, communicating well, exercising leadership, and team building (all subjects covered in individual chapters). But you should also pay attention to the specific techniques discussed below.

Planning
Coordination should take place before the event rather than after it. Planning is the first step. This means deciding what should be done and when. It is a process of dividing the total task into a number of sequenced or related sub-tasks. Then you work out priorities and time scales.

Organizing
You know what should be done. You then decide who does it. When you divide work between people you should avoid breaking apart those tasks which are linked together and which you cannot separate cleanly from each other.

Your biggest problem will be deciding where the boundaries between distinct but related activities should be. If the boundary is either too rigid or insufficiently well defined, you may have coordination problems. Don't rely too much upon the formal organization as defined in job descriptions, charts and manuals. If you do, you will induce inflexibility and set up communication barriers, and these are fatal to coordination.

The informal organization which exists in all companies can help coordination. When people work together they develop a system of social relationships which cut across formal organizational boundaries. They create a network of informal groups which tend to discipline themselves. This frees management from detailed supervision and control and leaves it more time for planning, problem solving and the overall monitoring of performance.

Delegating

The informal organization can help, but you still need to delegate work to individuals in a way that ensures they know what is expected of them *and* are aware of the need to liaise with others to achieve a coordinated result.

The art is to make everyone concerned understand the points on which they must link up with other people and the time in which such actions have to be completed. You should not have to *tell* people to coordinate, they should coordinate almost automatically. This they will do if you delegate not only specific tasks but also the job of working with others.

Communicating

You should not only communicate clearly what you want done, you should also encourage people to communicate with one another.

Avoid situations in which people can say: 'Why didn't someone tell me about this? If they had, I could have told them how to get out of the difficulty.' Nobody should be allowed to resort to James Forsyte's excuse that 'no one tells me anything'. It is up to people to find out what they need to know and not wait to be told.

Controlling

If you use the processes described above, and they work, theoretically you will not have to worry any more about coordination. But of course, life is not like that. You must monitor actions and results, spot problems and take swift corrective action when necessary. Coordination doesn't just happen. It has to be worked at, but avoid getting too involved. Allow people as much freedom as possible to develop horizontal relationships. These can facilitate coordination far more effectively than rigid and authoritarian control from above.

A case study

There is no one right way of coordinating a number of activities. It all depends on the nature of those activities and the circumstances in which they are carried out; for example, the present organization structure, the existence of coordinating committees and the facility with which communication can take place between those involved. Ultimately, good coordination depends upon the will of everyone concerned – to coordinate or be coordinated. Mechanical devices such as committees will not necessarily do the trick.

An example of good coordination took place in a company which was developing a new product in a new market. Neither the product nor the market fitted conveniently into the existing divisional structure and it was therefore decided to appoint one man as project manager to get the product launched. He would have a staff of two – a brand manager and a secretary. The work of development, production, marketing, selling and customer servicing would be carried out by the relevant departments in various divisions of the company.

The project manager had the status and authority to get things done by each department. The board was right behind the project and had allocated the priorities and resources required. But the different activities had to be coordinated and only the project manager could do it.

The easy way out would have been to set up a massive coordinating committee and leave it at that. This would have failed. Projects of this complexity cannot be coordinated just by creating a committee.

The project manager developed a different approach which proved to be highly successful. His first objective was to make everyone concerned enthusiastic about the project. He wanted them to believe in its importance so that they would be committed to working closely with the other departments involved.

His next step was to hold separate discussions with each departmental head so that he completely understood the programme of work required in each area. With the help of a project planner he then drew up a chart showing the key events and activities, and the relationships between them and the sequence in which they needed to take place in order to complete the project. This chart was distributed to all the departmental heads supplemented by an explanatory brief on the work required at each stage of the programme. Only then did he call a meeting to iron out difficulties and to ensure that everyone knew what had to be done and when.

He set up a system of progress reports and held progress meetings with departmental heads. But these were only held as necessary and he did not rely upon them to achieve coordination. He depended much more on personal contacts with individual managers, reviewing problems, noting where adjustments to the programme were needed, and stimulating the managers to even greater efforts when required. It was time consuming, but it kept him closely in touch so that he could anticipate any likely delays, setbacks or failures in communication, and be in a position to take action. He used the chart as his main instrument for checking that the critical events took place as planned.

The successful coordination and completion of the project were not achieved by one method but by the judicious use of a combination of techniques relevant to the situation: motivating, team building, planning, integrating, monitoring and controlling.

Chapter 11
Cost cutting

Costs always require to be controlled. You should start with the assumption that costs are too high and that they can be reduced. This assumption is based on the knowledge that some companies have not only survived but have flourished after drastic cost cutting exercises. When you remove the fat that always exists, you get a leaner and more powerful organization.

Cost cutting requires these basic approaches:

☐ Decide where and what to cut
☐ Plan to cut
☐ Conduct the cost reduction exercise.

What to cut

Your attack on costs should concentrate on these six areas:

☐ *Labour costs.* In labour intensive companies manpower costs may exceed 50 per cent of income. Overmanning, especially in service and staff departments is a major contributory cause of excessively high costs. Labour costs will include the direct costs of salaries, wages and benefits and the indirect cost of the personnel and training functions.
☐ *Manufacturing costs.* These are the actual costs incurred in making products; they reflect labour, material and operating costs but also, importantly, the way in which the product has been designed.
☐ *Selling costs.* These may be largely accounted for by the sales force which is covered under labour costs. But the figure will also include advertising, promotions, public relations, packaging and display material.
☐ *Development costs.* These are the costs of developing new products, markets, processes and materials, and of

67

acquiring new businesses.

☐ *Material and inventory costs.* The cost of buying materials and bought-in parts and of maintaining optimum stock levels.

☐ *Operating costs.* All the other costs incurred in operating the business. This will include space, computers, the provision of plant and equipment, paperwork systems and all the services required to keep the organization going.

Waste

Any examination of costs should aim to identify wasteful practices. The areas where they can occur need to be identified before conducting a cost reduction exercise so that attention can be directed to likely trouble spots. Concentrate both on company practices or procedures which lead to waste or pointless costs and on areas where staff can waste time or incur unnecessary expenditure.

The company can be wasteful in any or all of the following ways:

☐ Unnecessary forms or over-complex paperwork procedures
☐ Too much checking and verifying of work
☐ Too many and/or too large committees
☐ Too many layers of management
☐ Bottlenecks and inefficient work flows or procurement procedures
☐ Delays in decision making because authority is not delegated down the line
☐ Over rigid adherence to rules and regulations
☐ Too much committed to paper.

Time-wasting practices by staff include lateness or leaving early, prolonged tea or meal breaks, unnecessary breaks for any other reason, and dealing with personal matters in company time.

Cost-creating practices include absenteeism and frequent absence through illness (which may or may not be justified). Other wasteful practices include extravagant use of the company's facilities and equipment, such as photocopying machines, telephones and stationery.

Planning to cut costs

First, you build cost effectiveness into your plans, using value analysis techniques when you can. Then you introduce or improve procedures which define what costs you can incur and, at a later stage, control expenditure against budget. Zero-base budgeting, as described in Chapter 3, is a useful technique for taking every expense and 'shaking it' to make sure that it is justified.

Plans

Plans should be based on cost/benefit studies which aim to get the best ratio between expenditure and results, ie to minimize costs and maximize benefits. The emphasis should be on realism. It is good to be forward looking and entrepreneurial. But if you are like that, you are always in danger of becoming euphoric about the future, overestimating the benefits and underestimating the costs. At the planning stage you must be realistic about costs. Don't accept averages and assumed overhead rates. Get actuals. Find out what you are really going to spend and add at least 10 per cent for contingencies. Allow for inflation too.

You should be equally realistic about likely benefits. Do some 'sensitivity analysis' to determine the effects on profits and costs of optimistic, realistic and pessimistic forecasts of performance.

Design

Ensure that when products, systems or services are designed, at every stage the costs of what you are going to do are evaluated. Use value analysis techniques for this purpose.

Value analysis

Value analysis takes each part of the product, service or system, and subjects it to detailed examination to see if there is any way in which its cost could be reduced without affecting quality. You start with the assumption that anything you use or do can be bought, made or operated at less cost.

Value analysis in manufacturing is often carried out by a committee using brainstorming techniques to consider alternative, less costly ways of achieving the functions for which the article is being manufactured. These functions cover the use to which the article is being put and, therefore, consideration has to be given to marketing and pricing considerations as well as manufacturing costs. But, given a definition of use, the main aim of value analysis is to reduce the costs of materials, processing and labour. The following is a checklist of points to be covered.

1. Does its use contribute to value?
2. Is its cost proportionate to its usefulness?
3. Does it need all its features?
4. Is there a better alternative which will meet its intended use?
5. Can a usable part be made by a less costly method?
6. Can a standard and less costly part be used instead?
7. Will another dependable supplier provide it at less cost?
8. Can alternative and cheaper materials or components be used?
9. Can it be manufactured with the use of less skilled labour or less expensive machinery or equipment?
10. Can it be manufactured in a way which will reduce the number of standard labour hours required?
11. Can its design be simplified to reduce manufacturing costs?
12. Can the tolerances specified be modified to ease manufacture and reduce reject rates?

Although value analysis was first developed as a design engineering technique, the approach is equally applicable to the design of any system or service where the component parts can be costed.

The cost reduction exercise

A cost reduction exercise is a planned campaign aimed at cutting costs by a specified amount. It requires three steps:

☐ *Setting targets*, either for immediate cuts in crisis conditions or for specific reductions in the short term (defined in weeks rather than months). Targets may be set in specific areas, eg a 10 per cent cut in staff. Or they may be for a more comprehensive overhead reduction or a productivity increase.

The significant impact of overheads on profits should be emphasized to everyone. It is interesting to note that in a company with a turnover of £200,000 where profits are 10 per cent of sales, a reduction in the ratio of labour costs to sales from 11 to 10 per cent would increase profits by 10 per cent. It all ends up on the bottom line, and that is what counts.

Productivity targets expressed in financial terms, such as 'reduce costs per unit of output by 3 per cent', may be less immediate but they could usefully be incorporated in a set of cost reduction targets as longer-term objectives. Increases in productivity can be achieved by reducing costs in relation to output, or by increasing output in relation to costs or, preferably, by both reducing costs and increasing output (see Chapter 34). The message must be got across that unit costs are there to be attacked at all times — after all, they aggregate into total costs. Wherever possible, get down to basics — the shop floor and the general office. That is where the main costs are incurred. Keep it simple. Look at specific items. Use value analysis. Compare and contrast to identify places where costs are excessive.

□ *Deciding where to cut*, which will probably be in manpower costs or wasteful practices. It is remarkable how often departmental managers who scream with pain when they are told to cut their staff by 10 per cent cope quite well afterwards. O & M specialists will claim and prove that they can always cut staff numbers by 15 per cent without reducing efficiency.

With regard to wasteful or unnecessary practices, Sir Derek Rayner's campaign in Marks & Spencer illustrated what can be done. A drive on paperwork eliminated 26 million forms in annual use and cut the number of staff by 25 per cent.

□ *Deciding how to cut*: allocating responsibilities and then drawing up the programme and implementing it.

Responsibility for the cost reduction exercise
The most important thing to do is to appoint as senior an executive as possible, preferably a full-time member of the board, to direct the cost reduction exercise. He should have drive, energy, determination and, most importantly, the authority and courage to implement measures, however unpleasant some of them may be.

The question of who is to assist this executive then arises. You may consider using management consultants to help and give advice on specific problem areas. But do not ask consultants to carry out the main task. If your organization is not capable of taking action itself, however drastic, it does not deserve to survive.

Neither should you set up a committee to control the exercise. Committees are obstacles to action. You might set up a small (not more than three persons) project team of senior executives, but do not let them function as a standing committee with agenda, minutes and so on. Better still, give complete authority to one director to control the exercise, to use whom he wants when he wants and to call meetings as and when he thinks fit.

The director in charge of the exercise requires terms of reference by which to operate. These should normally take the form of a set of targets for him to achieve by a given date or sequence of dates. If there are any constraints (eg don't sack the chairman's son-in-law) he should be told them now. He should also be told the extent of his authority to make decisions and when and in what circumstances he should report back. He can then proceed to solicit opinions about what needs to be done, get the facts to support or refute the opinions, define the problem areas, decide what to do and draw up a programme for doing it.

Approach to the exercise
The highly successful cost reduction exercises conducted by Marks & Spencer used the most simple of questioning techniques:

☐ What is done?
☐ Why is it done?
☐ Does it need to be done at all?
☐ If it needs to be done, can it be simplified or carried out more cheaply?

The basis of the approach, to paraphrase Wittgenstein, was 'if anything needs to be done at all it can be done more simply'.

A number of other principles emerged from the Marks & Spencer experience which are universally applicable. These were summarized by Sir Derek Rayner as follows:

☐ *Top managers must accept a revision of the administrator's task.* Top management has imposed on administration countless rules and regulations to ensure that the systems and methods used in the business are foolproof. These have apparently been 'written largely on the assumption that all employees fall into two categories: stupid or crooked'. As Sir Derek wrote: 'If you cast the role of the administrator as bureaucrat he will perform it superbly.' The paraphernalia of administrative systems drawn up under this type of regime can only be swept away by top management.

- *The price of perfection is prohibitive: sensible approximation costs less.* Or, in Voltaire's words, 'the best is the enemy of the good'. Aim towards perfection, but don't overstretch yourself in achieving it. Productivity applied to administration means one man trying to achieve 95 per cent efficiency and reaching it, rather than two men trying to achieve 100 per cent and reaching perhaps 90 per cent.
- *Most employees can be trusted.* If this principle is accepted, a wide range of checks and monitoring can be discarded and replaced by managers managing and supervisors supervising. Thorough spot checks can be used to supplement day-to-day management.
- *All staff can help to bring about the desired changes.* Most people, if encouraged, will bring forward ideas to simplify and rationalize their work.
- *Staff can become too specialized.* Too many specialists create unnecessary work and hinder flexibility. 'Specialists exist to serve and ease the running of the business, not to stifle initiative, become barriers to action, and create yet another paper chain.'
- *Never legislate for every eventuality* but instead leave as much as possible to the common sense of those who are trusted in managerial positions.
- *There is no substitute for personal probing into what really happens.* 'You will find your most cherished documents and reports conceal a multitude of inaccuracies and omissions. Do not be afraid of only a sample first-hand investigation. It is often far more valuable than the all-embracing written one. And do not mistake for personal probing a meeting held in a private office.'

A case study

The policy pursued over a long period by Marks & Spencer is the best example of a company-wide programme for improving productivity by streamlining procedures and eliminating wasteful and unnecessary practices.

The main attack launched by Sir Derek Rayner in Marks & Spencer was on unnecessary paperwork, which generates unnecessary work and leads to the employment of superfluous labour.

The first campaign was fought in the late 1950s. Its purpose was not to achieve economies for economy's sake, but to make more effective use of resources. The campaign eliminated 26 million forms in annual use and progressively reduced the number of staff from 27,000 to 20,000. Yet Marks & Spencer continued to grow rapidly, doubling in size between 1963 and 1971.

An example of the improvements produced by the campaign was a complete change to the method of providing merchandising information to the stores. There was a detailed system of recording sales, stocks and requirements which was theoretically sound. Unfortunately, it took many people a great deal of time to digest the information and to act upon it. They were tied to paper and could not see the merchandise for the figures. The system was completely swept away and members of the staff were invited to pay more attention to the goods themselves, which, of course, they then had time to do. Very short summaries were now sent to head office and many simple ways of giving the stores a reasonably balanced supply of goods were developed.

Another key change was the reduction in the extent to which staff in the stores had become specialized, largely because of the forms and systems used. For example, there were many stock room specialists and the stock rooms were virtually isolated from the sales floor. Sales personnel had to fill up a form if they required stock for their counters. The stock was sorted out by a stock room specialist and eventually delivered to the counters. This practice was abolished and the stock room was thrown open to all, so that sales staff could simply go and replenish their counters. This not only saved time and paper and speeded up the supply of goods, but also paid an unexpected dividend in that the sales staff quickly became far more interested in their jobs.

Simultaneously with this drive on unnecessary paperwork, Marks & Spencer stopped recruitment. It became apparent in the early stages of the exercise that each stage in simplification meant that the system could work with fewer people. As simplification proceeded, the staff numbers steadily ran down by natural wastage. At the same time, people were redeployed from unproductive to productive work.

To win one battle, however, does not mean that you have won the war. As Sir Derek Rayner wrote in the *Harvard Business Review* (Jan-Feb 1975): 'Though our management believed it was alert to the dangers of excessive paperwork and overcomplication, the familiar signs of trouble began to reappear, for instance, fast-rising administrative expenses and ever-increasing demands for more staff. So in 1973, under the chairmanship of Sir Marcus Sieff, we mounted a new campaign known as 'Good Housekeeping'. Again the results were outstanding. Millions of pieces of paper in the shape of reports, forms and returns were eliminated. Thousands of hours spent on needless detail were saved. We reduced the staff from 27,000 people to 26,000 by not hiring replacements as employees left .... Most important, good housekeeping has freed our managers to spend more time on managing instead of interpreting the written word. It has enabled important staff members to get away more often from their desks and learn first hand what is going on in the stores and in supplier organizations.'

This campaign saved 200,000 forms a year by simplifying control of cash in tills. Stock control was simplified and the information needed by headquarters was cut by half a million pages a year. The investigating team dispensed with the 13 million forms used each year to process returned goods before the customer got his or her money back: why not they asked, meet legitimate claims at once from the till? The campaign reduced staff costs by 5 per cent, *and*, Sir Derek Rayner argues, it gave customers a better service.

Chapter 12

Creative thinking

Walter Bagehot wrote: 'It is often said that men are ruled by their imagination; but it would be truer to say that they are governed by the weakness of their imagination.'

Unimaginative management is a sure way to failure. Creative thinking aims to overcome the danger of being governed by this weakness.

Creative and logical thinking

Creative thinking is imaginative thinking. It produces new ideas, new ways of looking at things. It relates things or ideas which were previously unrelated. It is discontinuous and divergent. Edward de Bono invented the phrase 'lateral thinking' for it and this term has stuck; it implies sideways leaps in the imagination rather than a continuous progression down a logical chain of reasoning.

Logical or analytical thinking is a step-by-step process. It is continuous, one step leading to the next until, ideally, you converge on the only possible solution. It is sometimes called 'convergent' thinking; de Bono refers to it as 'vertical thinking' because you go straight down the line from one state of information to another.

De Bono summed up the differences between vertical and lateral thinking as follows:

Vertical thinking	*Lateral thinking*
Chooses	Changes
Looks for what is right	Looks for what is different
One thing must follow directly from another	Makes deliberate jumps

Vertical thinking	*Lateral thinking*
Concentrates on relevance	Welcomes chance intrusions
Moves in the most likely directions	Explores the least likely

Creative thinking is not superior to logical thinking. It's just different. The best managers are both creative and logical. Eventually, however creative they have been, they have to make a decision. And logical thinking is necessary to ensure that it is the right decision.

The process of creativity

In *The Act of Creation* Arthur Koestler described the process of creativity as one of 'bisociation'; putting together two unconnected facts or ideas to form a single idea. The establishment of the relationship or bisociation is usually accompanied by a release of tension. There is a flash of illumination leading to a shout of 'Eureka!' or at least 'Aha!'. As Koestler remarks, it is like the release of tension after the unexpected punch line of a joke — the 'haha' reaction. Or even the less dramatic release of tension when confronting a work of art.

If we assume that it is desirable to increase our capacity for creative thinking, then there are three things to do:

1. Understand the barriers to creative thinking
2. Develop individual capacity for creative thinking
3. Use the collective capacities of groups of people to develop new ideas by 'brainstorming'.

Barriers to creative thinking

The main barriers to creative thinking are:

□ Allowing your mind to be conditioned into following a dominant pattern — the mind is a patterning system and this means you can be trapped into a fixed way of looking at things, what de Bono calls a 'concept prison', or a 'tethering factor'
□ Restricting the free growth of your ideas within rigidly drawn boundaries which are treated as limiting conditions
□ Failure to identify and examine the assumptions you are making to ensure that they are not restricting the

development of new ideas
- [ ] Polarizing alternatives — reducing every decision to an 'either/or' when there may be other ways of looking at things
- [ ] Being conditioned to think sequentially rather than laterally and looking for the 'best' idea, not different ideas. As de Bono says: 'It is better to have enough ideas for some of them to be wrong than always to be right by having no ideas at all.'
- [ ] Lack of effort in challenging the obvious — it is tempting to slip into the easy solution
- [ ] Evaluating too quickly — jumping to conclusions and not giving yourself enough time to allow your imagination to range freely over other possible ways of looking at things
- [ ] A tendency to conform — to give the answer expected
- [ ] Fear of looking foolish or being put down.

How to develop your ability to think creatively

If you want to think more creatively, the first thing to do is to analyse yourself. Go through the list of barriers to creativity and ask yourself the question, 'Is this me?' If it is, then think about ways in which you can overcome the difficulty, concentrating on:

- [ ] Breaking away from any restrictions
- [ ] Opening up your mind to generate new ideas
- [ ] Delaying judgement until you have thoroughly explored the alternative ideas.

Breaking away
To break away from the constraints on your ability to generate new ideas you should:

- [ ] Identify the dominant ideas influencing your thinking
- [ ] Define the boundaries (ie past experience, precedents, policies, procedures, rules) within which you are working and try to get outside them by asking questions such as:

  — Are the constraints reasonable?
  — Is past experience reliable?
  — What's new about the present situation?
  — Is there another way?

- [ ] Bring your assumptions out into the open and challenge any which restrict your freedom to develop new ideas

☐ Reject 'either/or' propositions – ask, 'Is there really a simple choice between alternatives?'

☐ Keep on asking 'Why?' (But bear in mind that if you do this too bluntly to other people you can antagonize them.)

Generating new ideas

To generate new ideas you have to open up your mind. If you have removed some of the constraints as suggested above you will be in a better position to:

☐ Look at the situation differently, exploring all possible angles

☐ List as many alternative approaches as possible without seeking the 'one best way' (there is no such thing) and without indulging in premature evaluation (which can only lead to partial satisfaction)

☐ In de Bono's words, 'arrange discontinuity', deliberately set out to break the mould. The techniques for triggering off new ideas include:

— Free thinking, allowing your mind to wander over alternative and in many cases apparently irrelevant ways of looking at the situation

— Deliberately exposing yourself to new influences in the form of people, articles, books, indeed anything which might give you a different insight, even though it might not be immediately relevant

— Switching yourself or other people from problem to problem

— Arranging for the cross-fertilization of ideas with other people

— Using analogies to spark off ideas. The analogy should be suggested by the problem but should then be allowed to exist in its own right to indicate a different way of looking at the problem.

Delaying judgement

Your aim in creative thinking should be to separate the evaluation of ideas from their generation. The worst mistake you can make is to kill off new ideas too quickly. It is always easy to find ten ways of saying 'no' to anything. For example:

☐ It won't work

☐ We're already doing it

- ☐ It's been tried before without success
- ☐ It's not practical
- ☐ It won't solve the problem
- ☐ It's too risky
- ☐ It's based on pure theory
- ☐ It will cost too much
- ☐ It will antagonize the customers/the boss/the union/the workers/the shareholders, etc
- ☐ It will create more problems than it solves.

Some of these objections may be valid. But they should be held back until you have generated as many ideas as possible. Allow ideas to grow a little. Don't strangle them at birth.

It is too easy to say 'no', too easy to ridicule anything new or different. In creative thinking it is the end result that counts, and if you want it to be original you must not worry too much about the route you follow to get there. It doesn't matter if you stumble sometimes or take the wrong turning, as long as delays are not protracted and you arrive in the right place at the end.

As de Bono says:

> In vertical thinking one has to be right at every step. So, no matter how many steps are taken, the end point (idea, solution, conclusion) is automatically right if all the intervening steps have been right . . . . In lateral thinking one does not *have* to be right at each step, but one must be right at the *end*.

Delaying judgement is difficult. It goes against the grain. You have to make a conscious effort to hold back until the right moment arrives, which is when you feel that you have collected as many new ideas as you can in the time available.

Our training, our inhibitions, our reluctance to look foolish or to go out on a limb all work against us. We should certainly try to do it ourselves and persuade other people to go along with us. But we can help the processes of opening up, introducing discontinuity and releasing new ideas by the technique of brainstorming.

Brainstorming

Brainstorming has been defined as a means of getting a large number of ideas from a group of people in a short time. It is essentially a group activity which uses a formal setting to generate as many ideas as possible without pausing to evaluate them.

The main features of a brainstorming session are:

1. A group of between six and twelve people is assembled. Some will be directly involved with the problem, some should be drawn from other areas from which they can bring different ideas and experience to bear on the problem. There is a chairman and a note-taker.
2. The chairman defines the rules, emphasizing that:
    — The aim is to get as many ideas as possible
    — No attempt will be made to evaluate any ideas
    — No one should feel inhibited about coming up with suggestions.
3. If necessary there is a warm-up session to familiarize the group with the procedure. For example, they could be asked to suggest how many uses they can think of for a paper clip.
4. The chairman states the problem, avoiding the trap of defining it too narrowly.
5. The chairman opens the session by a phrase such as 'In how many ways can we . . . ?'
6. The chairman encourages people to contribute and prevents any attempt to evaluate ideas. From time to time he may restate the problem.
7. The note-taker condenses the ideas suggested and lists them on flip charts. He does not attempt to act as an editor or worry about duplications at this stage. The session should not be tape recorded as this may inhibit ideas.
8. The chairman keeps on encouraging the group to contribute, trying to get people to freewheel and produce as many ideas as possible — good, bad, indifferent, sensible or silly. He keeps the pace going and never comments or allows anyone else to comment on a contribution. Every idea is treated as relevant.
9. The chairman closes the meeting after 30 minutes or so — 45 minutes at most. The session must not be allowed to drag on.
10. Evaluation takes place later, possibly with a different group. At this session the aim is to:
    — Select ideas for immediate use
    — Identify ideas for further exploration
    — Review any different approaches which have been revealed by the session.

Brainstorming is a useful technique for releasing ideas, over-coming inhibitions, cross-fertilizing ideas and getting away from patterned thinking. It needs to be planned and executed carefully and proper evaluation is essential.

Use it selectively, where there seems to be ample scope for different ideas. It will not solve all your problems but can help you to crash through the barriers erected by the traditional approaches to decision making.

Remember that however creative you are, what you finally decide on has to work. Brainstorming and other techniques for increasing creativity will help you to break new ground, but eventually you will have to think clearly and analytically about the pros and cons of the preferred solution before making your final decision.

Chapter 13
Delegation

You can't do everything yourself, so you have to delegate. At first sight delegation looks simple. Just tell someone what you want him to do and then let him do it. But there is more to it than that.

It may be that you would wish to delegate everything except what your subordinate cannot do. But you cannot then withdraw. You have arranged for someone else to do the job, but you have not passed on the responsibility for it. You are always accountable to your superior for what your subordinate does. Hence, as is often said, you can't delegate responsibility.

Delegation is difficult. It is perhaps the hardest thing that managers have to do. The problem is getting the balance right between delegating too much or too little and between over- or under- supervision. When you give someone something to do you have to make sure that it gets done. And you have to do that without breathing down his neck, wasting your time and his, and getting in the way. There has to be trust as well as guidance and supervision.

Advantages of delegation

- [ ] It relieves you of routine and less critical tasks
- [ ] It frees you for more important work — planning, organizing, motivating and controlling
- [ ] It extends your capacity to manage
- [ ] It reduces delay in decision making — as long as authority is delegated close to the point of action
- [ ] It allows decisions to be taken at the level where the details are known
- [ ] It develops the capacity of staff to make decisions, get things done and take responsibility.

When to delegate

You should delegate when:

☐ You have more work than you can effectively carry out yourself
☐ You cannot allocate sufficient time to your priority tasks
☐ You want to develop your subordinate
☐ The job can be done adequately by your subordinate.

How to delegate

When you delegate you have to decide:

☐ What to delegate
☐ To whom you delegate — choosing who does the work
☐ How to inform or brief your subordinate — giving out the work
☐ How you will guide and develop your subordinate
☐ How you will monitor his performance.

What to delegate
You delegate tasks that you don't need to do yourself. You are not just ridding yourself of the difficult, tedious or unrewarding tasks. Neither are you trying to win for yourself an easier life. Delegation will, in fact, make your life more difficult, but also more rewarding.

Clearly, you delegate routine and repetitive tasks which you cannot reasonably be expected to do yourself — as long as you use the time you have won productively.

You also delegate specialist tasks to those who have the skills and know-how to do them. You cannot do it all yourself. Nor can you be expected to know it all yourself. You have to know how to select and use expertise. There will be no problem as long as you make it clear what you want from the experts and ask — if necessary force — them to present it to you in a usable way. As a manager you must know what the specialist can do for you and you should be knowledgeable enough about the subject to understand whether or not what they produce is worth having.

Choosing who does the work
Ideally, the person you choose to do the work should have the knowledge, skills, motivation and time needed to get it done to your complete satisfaction. Frequently, however, you will have

to use someone who has less than ideal experience, knowledge or skills. In these cases you should try to select an individual who has intelligence, natural aptitude and, above all, willingness to learn how to do the job with help and guidance. This is how people develop, and the development of your staff should be your conscious aim whenever you delegate.

You are looking for someone you can trust. You don't want to over-supervise, so you have to believe that the person you select will get on with it and have the sense to come to you if he is stuck or before he makes a bad mistake.

How do you know whom you can trust? The best way is to try people out first on smaller and less important tasks, increasingly giving them more scope so that they learn how far they can go and you can observe how they do it. If they get on well, their sense of responsibility and powers of judgement will increase and improve and you will be able to trust them with more demanding and responsible tasks.

Giving out the work
When you delegate you should ensure that your subordinate understands:

☐ Why the work needs to be done
☐ What he is expected to do
☐ The date by which he is expected to do it
☐ The authority he has to make decisions
☐ The problems he must refer back
☐ The progress or completion reports he should submit
☐ How you propose to guide and monitor him
☐ The resources and help he will have to get the work done.

Your subordinate may need guidance on how the work should be done. The extent to which you spell it out will clearly depend on how much he already knows about how to do the work. You don't want to give directions in such laborious detail that you run the risk of stifling your subordinate's initiative. As long as you are sure he will get the job done without breaking the law, exceeding his budget, embarrassing you or seriously upsetting people, let him get on with it. Follow Robert Heller's golden rule: 'If you can't do something yourself, find someone who can — and then let him do it in his own sweet way.'

You can make a distinction between *hard* and *soft* delegation. Hard delegation takes place when you tell someone exactly what to do, how to do it and when you want the results. You spell it out, confirm it in writing and make a note in your diary of the date when you expect the job to be completed. And then you follow up regularly.

Soft delegation takes place when you agree generally what has to be achieved and leave your subordinate to get on with it. You should still agree limits of authority, define the decisions to be referred to you, say what exception reports you want (see Chapter 9), and indicate when and how you will review progress. Then you sit back until the results are due and observe from afar, only coming closer for periodical progress meetings, or when the exception reports suggest that something needs looking into, or when a problem or decision is referred to you.

You should always delegate by the results you expect. Even if you do not need to specify *exactly* how the results should be achieved, it is a good idea when delegating a problem to ask your subordinate to tell you how he proposes to solve it. You then have the opportunity to provide guidance at the outset; guidance at a later stage may be seen as interference.

Guidance and development
Delegation not only helps you to get your work done; it can be used to improve your subordinate's performance and therefore your trust in his ability to carry out more responsible work. Instruction, training and development are part of the process of delegation.

Monitoring performance
At first you may have to monitor a subordinate's performance carefully. But the sooner you can relax and watch progress informally the better.

You will have set target dates, and you should keep a reminder of these in your diary so that you can ensure they are achieved. Don't allow your subordinates to become careless about meeting deadlines.

Without being oppressive, you should ensure that progress reports are made when required and that you discuss deviations from the original plan in good time. You will have clearly indicated to your subordinate the extent of his authority to act without further reference to yourself. He must therefore expect to be reprimanded if on any occasion he exceeds his brief or fails to keep you informed. You don't want any surprises and your subordinate must understand that you will not tolerate being kept in the dark.

Try to restrain yourself from undue interference with the way the work is being done. It is, after all, the results that count. Of course you must step in if there is any danger of things going off the rails. The Nelson touch is all right if your subordinate is a Nelson, but how many Nelsons have you got? Rash decisions, over-expenditure and ignoring defined and reasonable constraints and rules must be prevented.

There is a delicate balance to be achieved between hedging someone around with restrictions which may appear petty and allowing him licence to do what he likes. You must use your knowledge of the subordinate and the circumstances to decide where the balance should be struck. The best delegators are those who have a comprehensive understanding of the strengths and weaknesses of their staff and the situation in which they are working.

Above all, avoid 'river banking'. This happens when a boss gives his subordinate a task which is more or less impossible to do. As the subordinate is 'going down' for the third time his boss is observed in a remote and safe position on the river bank saying: 'It's easy really, all you need to do is to try a bit harder.'

The thoughts of some successful delegators

John H. Johnson, editor and publisher of Johnson Publishing Company, chief executive officer of Supreme Life Insurance Company and on the board of many large US corporations said of his delegation techniques: 'I want to be big and I want to be bigger and I can't do it all by myself. So I try to do only those things that I can't get anyone else to do.'

Franklin D. Roosevelt used a particularly ruthless technique based on competition, when he requested his aides to find some information. One of his aides told the story as follows: 'He would call you in, and he'd ask you to get the story on some complicated business and you'd come back after a couple of days of hard labour and present the juicy morsel you'd uncovered under a stone somewhere and *then* you'd find out he knew all about it, along with something else you *didn't* know. Where he got this information from he wouldn't mention, usually, but after he had done this to you once or twice you got damn careful about your information.'

Robert Townsend's approach to delegation when he was chairman of Avis was to emphasize the need to delegate 'as many important matters as you can because that creates a climate in which people grow'.

Robert Magaven, when he started as the head of Safeway Food Stores told his division managers: 'I don't know anything about the grocery business but you fellows do. From now on, you're running your division as if it were your own business. You don't take orders from anyone but me and I'm not going to give you orders. I'm going to hold you responsible.'

Franklin Moore related the following example of strong delegation: Ralf Cordiner, the head of General Electric in the US for ten years had a vice president who wanted to see him urgently about a problem. The vice president explained his problem, and the choices he thought he had. 'Now, Mr Cordiner,' he said, 'What should I do?' 'Do?' Cordiner answered, 'You'd damn well better get on an airplane and get back to your office and decide. And if you can't decide we'd better get someone who can.'

Peter Drucker, writing about responsibility, referred to a newspaper interview with a young American infantry captain in the Vietnam jungle. The reporter asked: 'How in this confused situation can you retain command?' The captain replied: 'Around here, I am the only guy who is responsible. If these men don't know what to do when they run into an enemy in the jungle, I'm too far away to tell them. My job is to make sure they know. What they do depends on the situation which only they can judge. The responsibility is always mine, but the decision lies with whoever is on the spot.'

A case study

A group of researchers studying how managers delegate found that the following was happening in one of the companies they were studying:

In the situations in which the men we were interviewing found themselves, the boss was usually a hurried, and sometimes a harried, man. He gave out broad, briefly stated assignments, expecting his subordinates to make sense out of them. He also expected them to decide what information they needed, to get that information and then to go ahead and carry out their assignments. In the case of repetitive tasks, the typical boss assumed that after a few trials his subordinates would know for themselves when a job needed doing.

Frequently the boss wasn't sure himself about which things needed attention in his department. And although he knew what eventually had to be accomplished, often he had less idea than his subordinates about the approaches to take. It wasn't unusual therefore for the boss to be vague or even impatient when approached with questions about the job while it was going on. Usually he was much more assertive in describing what he wanted after a job was done than while it was in progress.

The production director came out of the board of directors' meeting where he had been roundly criticized for not getting the most out of his organization. He immediately called a meeting of his subordinates and told them: 'I don't intend to subject myself to such humiliation again. You men are paid to do your jobs; it's not up to me to do them for you. I don't know how you spend your time and I don't intend to try to find out. You know your responsibilities, and these figures bear out that you haven't discharged them properly. If the next report doesn't show a marked improvement, there will be some new faces around here.'

Chapter 14
Developing people

Investing in people

The chairman of an advertising firm once said that his 'inventory goes up and down in the lift'. His prime resource — his working capital — was people. The same applies in any other sort of organization. Money matters, but the human beings who work there matter even more.

If you want to take a pragmatic view of people, regard them as an investment. They cost money to acquire and maintain and they should provide a return on that outlay; their value increases as they become more effective in their jobs and capable of taking on greater responsibility. In accounting terms, people may be treated like any other asset on the balance sheet, taking into account acquisition costs and their increasing value as they gain experience.

The learning curve

The rate at which the value of staff increases is related to their natural ability, their motivation and the opportunities they have to get jobs or to achieve promotion. Developing people is about accelerating the rate of this increase at minimum cost. It always takes a period of time to become effective in a job. This process can be represented by a 'learning curve', thus:

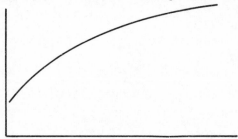

A career is often a sequence of learning curves, which could be represented thus (where x = promotion):

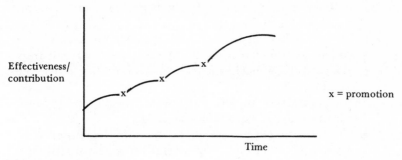

Development aims

Your aims should be:

1. To steepen the learning curve, ie to reduce the time taken to become effective
2. To minimize learning costs — the opportunity costs of what people could do if they were fully trained, and the actual cost of training them
3. To improve performance in the existing job, thus developing potential for the future.

To achieve these aims:

☐ Use systematic training techniques (for the manual and clerical jobs)
☐ Consciously plan the development of your present and future managers
☐ Take every opportunity you can to coach your staff to improve their present performance and develop potential. This is particularly important in the case of potential management material.

Training

Start by defining training needs, and on the basis of this definition decide how and where training is to be carried out.

Defining training needs
A training need exists when there is a gap between what someone *can* do and what he *should* be able to do. Training should be designed to fill that gap. The following steps should then be

taken to define training needs:

1. Identify overall corporate requirements for manpower and skills by studying the implications of expansion plans or changes in technology.
2. Identify other corporate requirements by analysing operating problems to establish whether they result from inadequacies in performance which would be corrected by training.
3. Use job analysis to define the requirements of individual jobs in terms of skills and knowledge.
4. Use performance assessment to measure the extent to which individuals or groups of individuals have gaps in knowledge or skills which could be corrected by training.
5. Determine individual training needs on the basis of performance appraisal and study the results of such appraisals to identify common training needs.
6. Carry out assessments of management succession requirements and the potential of individuals for promotion.

How to train — manual and clerical staff
For manual and clerical jobs where the knowledge and skill requirements are not too complex, job instruction techniques should be used. These should be based on job analysis, which breaks the job into stages, listing at each stage the operations that have to be performed and the skills and knowledge required. The key points to be learned should be emphasized, including special points of difficulty, safety factors and exceptions to the normal routines.

From this analysis you should draw up an instruction plan consisting of the following:

1. Put the trainee at ease and create interest by explaining why training is going to take place, what is going to be done and how the trainee will benefit from it.
2. Check on what the trainee already knows or can do.
3. Explain and, wherever possible, demonstrate what has to be done and how. Take one step at a time and only move on to the next step when you are sure the trainee has absorbed what has been taught. Stress key points and say and show everyting clearly.
4. Check understanding at each stage. Make the trainee do the work or explain to you what needs to be done.

5. Make the trainee practise each stage until the required standards of accuracy and speed are reached. It is sometimes best to do this progressively. Thus when any two successive stages can be done separately at the required standard, get the trainee to practise them jointly until the standard for both stages together is reached. Then a third part is added and so on until the whole job is learned.

6. Put the trainee to work, but check, evaluate and retrain as necessary.

Remember that the basic purpose of training is the transfer of skills from those who have them to those who do not. Just having the skills is not enough to be an effective trainer. Anyone responsible for training should understand how best to impart knowledge or skills using the techniques described above.

Remember also that when you are training someone, the person under instruction does not necessarily want to learn, and may even be frightened of learning. Hence the importance of putting trainees at ease and creating their interest in learning. They have to see it as something that will benefit them as well as the company. They must not feel threatened.

Where to train
Robert Townsend's approach to training in *Up the Organization* is simple: 'The only way I know to get somebody trained is on the job.'

This statement expresses a fundamental truth. People learn best by doing. Training off the job is too often irrelevant and there is always the problem of transferring what is learned on a course back to the workplace. Effective transfer of learning is possible if the off-the-job training simulates working conditions with a reasonable degree of precision, but this is often difficult to accomplish.

Training off the job is, however, appropriate in some circumstances. For example, it is often quicker and cheaper to train fitters and machinists in their basic skills in a separate workshop. And some knowledge, for example, of how to operate a new machine, may only be obtainable outside the organization.

But the fact remains that most learning takes place on the job, and its effectiveness depends on whether managers and supervisors are able to carry out training as one of their key responsibilities.

How to train managers

Off-the-job training can be of benefit to managers and supervisors. Action-centred techniques which involve trainees directly in real work problems, while providing them with the help and guidance of external tutors, have proved effective.

Managers can also benefit from the broadening effect of an external course which enables them to reflect and build upon their own experience and, more importantly, to meet and talk with other managers. Don't worry if they come back and say they learned more in the bar than in the classroom. It's what they learn that matters, not how they learn it.

Nevertheless, on-the-job training is still the best way of developing managers, especially if it is properly organized. Use planned experience and coaching as described below.

Management development

Management development is about improving the performance of existing managers, giving them opportunities for growth and development, and ensuring, as far as possible, that management succession is provided for.

Managers need to be given the opportunity to develop themselves. As Peter Drucker wrote:

> Development is always self-development. Nothing could be more absurd than for the enterprise to assume responsibility for the development of a man. The responsibility rests with the individual, his abilities, his efforts . . . . Every manager in a business has the opportunity to encourage self-development or to stifle it, to direct it or to misdirect it. He should be specifically assigned the responsibility for helping all men working with him to focus, direct and apply their self-development efforts productively. And every company can provide systematic development challenges to its managers.

In Douglas McGregor's phrase, managers are grown — they are neither born nor made. And your role is to provide conditions favourable to faster growth. As McGregor wrote:

> The job environment of the individual is the most important variable affecting his development. Unless that environment is conducive to his growth, none of the other things we do to him or for him will be effective. That is why the 'agricultural' approach to management development is preferable to the 'manufacturing' approach. The latter leads, among other things, to the unrealistic expectations that we can create and develop managers in the class room.

There are three main activities in management development — performance appraisal and management by objectives, both of which are discussed in Chapter 2, and planned experience.

Planned experience

People learn mainly through experience. Surely, therefore, it is worth spending a little of your time planning the experience of anyone with potential for development.

Planning someone's experience means giving him extra tasks to do which provide a challenge or extend him into a new area. It could be a project which he has to complete himself or he could be included in a project team looking at a new development or problem which cuts across organizational boundaries. Projects which enlarge experience in unfamiliar areas, for example a marketing executive in finance or vice versa, are particularly useful. Planned experience will work better if it is accompanied by coaching so that those undergoing it can receive the maximum benefit from expert advice.

Coaching

The best way to learn how to manage is to manage, under the guidance of a good manager. Coaching is an informal but deliberate way of providing this guidance. It should be linked to performance appraisal and the counselling that takes place as part of the appraisal procedure.

But coaching is a more continuous process. Every time you delegate a task to someone and discuss the outcome you are presented with a coaching opportunity. When you delegate you can provide guidance on how the job should be done. When you discuss progress with your subordinate or when he reports back to you, you can ask questions on how well he has thought through what he is doing, suggest alternative ways of looking at a problem (do not provide the solution) and provide constructive criticism if things are not going right.

You can help to develop people by discussing higher-level problems with them, involving them in your decisions and increasing their understanding of how to tackle a job senior to the areas for which they are responsible.

Every contact you have with a subordinate provides you with a coaching opportunity. Without too much effort, you can contribute significantly to his improvement and growth by making the most of the chances offered to you.

Chapter 15
Efficiency and effectiveness

In *Summer Lightning*, P. G. Wodehouse dubs Lord Emsworth's secretary 'the efficient Baxter'. He explains:

> We have called Rupert Baxter efficient and efficient he was. The word, as we interpret it, implies not only a capacity for performing the ordinary tasks of life with a smooth firmness of touch, but in addition a certain alertness of mind, a genius for opportunism, a genius for seeing clearly, thinking swiftly and Doing it Now.

Efficiency, as thus defined, is obviously an excellent characteristic. It includes the notion of effectiveness which is often emphasized less than it should be in the quest for efficiency.

Peter Drucker pointed out forcibly that to concentrate on efficiency rather than effectiveness could be limiting and, therefore dangerous. He wrote:

> Management, we are usually told, should concern itself with efficiency, that is with doing better what is already being done. It should therefore focus on costs. But the entrepreneurial approach focuses on effectiveness, that is, on the decision what to do. It focuses on opportunities to produce revenue, to create markets and to change the economic characteristics of existing products and markets. It asks not: how do we do this or that? It asks: which of the products really produce extraordinary economic results or are capable of producing them? Which of the markets and/or uses are capable of producing extraordinary results? It then asks: to what results should therefore the resources and efforts of the business be allocated so as to produce extraordinary results rather than the 'ordinary' ones which is all efficiency possibly can produce.

Developing this theme, Bill Reddin suggested that the manager who concentrates on efficiency instead of effectiveness tends to:

☐ Do things right rather than do right things
☐ Solve problems rather than produce creative alternatives
☐ Safeguard resources rather than optimize resource utilization

☐ Lower costs rather than increase profit.

The danger of laying too much emphasis on efficiency is that the object of the exercise becomes obscured by the bureaucratic machinery set up to achieve it. You should aim — in Drucker's phrase again — to manage for results. Clearly you adopt the most efficient way of getting there but never forget that it is the end that counts, not the means.

Case studies

In an insurance company the 'efficiency' of inspectors (ie sales representatives) was measured by the number of policies they sold and the volume of premium income they generated. Naturally, they concentrated on selling the easiest forms of policy and generated lots of income. But volume, while a measure of efficiency, did not indicate effectiveness, which could only be assessed by the relative profitability of the different policies. Without guidance on which policies were most profitable the inspectors were efficient in volume terms but ineffective in terms of the only true measure of performance, profitability.

The accounts department prided itself on the efficiency with which it delivered voluminous printouts analysing costs incurred against budget for each cost centre within two weeks of the end of the month. But the information was not effective in that it did not help cost centre managers to control some of their crucial costs. This was because so many items were accrued (ie assumptions were made about expenditure because invoices had not yet been processed) that many of the figures in key expenditure areas were meaningless. As a result, cost centre managers maintained their own sets of duplicate accounts.

The chairman of an Industrial Training Board which collected training levies from firms in the industry and redistributed them in the form of grants for approved training was concerned because levy income was exceeding grant expenditure. Many of the firms in the industry complained bitterly that the Training Board was accumulating vast useless reserves at their expense. The chairman therefore launched a nationwide campaign under the slogan 'Get your whack back Jack', encouraging firms to do training and claim levy. With great efficiency the firms in the industry completed forms by the dozen, making grant claims

97

for all sorts of training. But much of the training was irrelevant and for show.

A direct mail company decided to set up a 'party plan' type of operation to sell its products. It had no previous experience in this activity. Demonstrators had to be recruited, and it was decided that the current mailing list of people who had already shown some interest in the products would prove to be the best source of recruits. This seemed a less haphazard approach than advertising for demonstrators. The recruitment campaign was planned meticulously and executed with the utmost efficiency. Everything was thought of and everything happened as planned *except* that hardly anyone responded. The method proved to be totally ineffective because it was based on an incorrect assumption. The only ways to get good party plan demonstrators are by direct contact and classified advertising in the local press. An enquiry into why the mailing list members had not responded showed that the written approach through the mail failed to overcome their natural suspicions about party plan.

A government agency responsible for the recruitment of large numbers of staff had its procedures examined by an organization and methods team. It was noted that there were a number of directors of recruitment each responsible for particular 'competitions' to get different categories of staff. Each director had a group of staff to administer the various stages of a competition. But there was duplication of work such as the sifting and acknowledgement of applications, between the various directorates. The O & M team therefore hit on the 'efficient' solution, which was to have a number of units dealing with different activities: sifting, acknowledging, obtaining references, etc. Each of these units provided a service to all directors of recruitment but were controlled separately by a director of administration. This solution was certainly efficient in that it grouped associated activities together and saved staff. But it was also ineffective. Because there was no one person responsible for the control and coordination of individual competitions (the directors of recruitment sat on the sidelines as far as administration was concerned), delays took place at each stage. Competitions took much longer to complete and good recruits were being lost because they got tired of waiting.

An engineering firm ran into hard times and decided that a general cut of 20 per cent in all indirect staff was required.

A senior manager was appointed to implement the cut. He conducted the assignment with great efficiency. Everyone was quite clear about what they had to do, the programme was implemented exactly as planned and documentation was precise and complete. But the decision to make an all round 20 per cent cut had repercussions which had not been fully appreciated when the plans were made. A number of key research departments employing only indirect staff found that they had to dismiss key employees to achieve their targets. Their ability to provide for the longer-term development of the business was therefore seriously affected. The assignment was conducted efficiently but led to a significant decline in effectiveness where it really mattered — the future.

Chapter 16
Getting on

I am a young executive. No cuffs than mine are cleaner;
I have a Slimline brief-case and I use the firm's Cortina.
In every roadside hostelry from here to Burgess Hill
The maîtres d'hôtel all know me well and let me sign the bill.

You ask me what it is I do. Well, actually, you know,
I'm partly a liaison man and partly PRO
Essentially I integrate the current export drive
And basically I'm viable from ten o'clock till five.

(John Betjeman, *Collected Poems*, John Murray (Publishers) Ltd)

Getting on should not necessarily mean that you aspire to become like Betjeman's executive. But we do want to get on somewhere. The question is, how to do it? The traditional starting point is to 'know thyself'. Carlyle, however, describing this as an 'impossible precept', felt that to 'know what thou cans't work at' would be better advice. Getting on is first about knowing what you can do — your strengths and weaknesses. Then you can decide what you want to do and set out to do it.

You can start in the right direction, therefore, by trying to analyse yourself and the situation which you are in.

Beyond that there are certain actions you can take which will help you to get on. Some are obvious, others less so. How you apply them must depend on your assessment of where you are and what you can do. With due acknowledgement to the two men who have written the most sense on this subject — Peter Drucker and Robert Townsend — the list of things to do is set out below under three main headings:

- ☐ Knowing what you want
- ☐ Developing and deploying the skills required to get what you want
- ☐ Displaying the personal qualities and behaving in the ways that will contribute to your success.

100

Knowing what you want

1. Find out what you are good at doing and then do it.
2. Analyse not only your strengths but also your weaknesses: 'There is nothing that helps a man in his conduct through life more than a knowledge of his own characteristic weaknesses' (William Hazlitt).
3. Decide what you want to do and then go for it. Believe that if you really want something you can get it, and act accordingly.
4. Set demanding targets and deadlines for yourself. 'People grow according to the demands they make on themselves' (Drucker). But don't over-commit yourself. Be realistic about what you can achieve.
5. Pursue excellence. 'If you can't do it excellently don't do it at all' (Townsend).
6. Focus on what *you* can contribute. 'To ask "what can I contribute?" is to look for the unused potential in a job' (Drucker).
7. Get your priorities right. Adapt Drucker's rules for identifying them:
   — pick the future as against the past
   — focus on opportunities rather than on problems
   — choose your own direction — rather than climb on the bandwagon
   — aim high, aim for something that will make a difference rather than something that is 'safe' and easy to do.
8. Be specific about what you want to do yourself and what you want others to do for you.
9. Keep it simple. Concentrate. Consider all your tasks and eliminate the irrelevant ones. Slough off old activities before you start new ones. 'Concentration is the key to economic results . . . no other principle of effectiveness is violated as constantly today as the basic principle of concentration . . . . Our motto seems to be: "let's do a little bit of everything" ' (Drucker).
10. Take the broad view but don't ignore the significant detail: 'Ill can he rule the great, that cannot reach the small' (Spenser). It is sometimes necessary to penetrate beneath the surface to find out what is really happening — on the shop floor or in the field. But do this selectively.
11. Adapt to changing demands. 'The executive who keeps on doing what he has done successfully before is almost bound to fail' (Drucker).

Develop skills

Every chapter in this book refers to an area of management skill that you need to develop if you want to get on. The key areas are:

- [ ] Communicating — express yourself clearly, concisely and persuasively.
- [ ] Problem solving — adopt a logical approach to problem solving but don't forget that lateral thinking can be very productive of new ideas.
- [ ] Decision making — develop the analytical skills and confidence in yourself to enable you to make incisive judgements.
- [ ] Listening — listen to ideas and act on the good ones. Hear what is said, let the other person know that you have heard, show an interest, let him feel important.
- [ ] Motivating — understand what your people can do and what makes them tick, make clear what you expect them to do, setting standards which are grounded on the requirement of the task and are not personal, reward them or otherwise according to their contribution.
- [ ] Staffing — select people for their strengths, accept that everyone has some weakness or other, don't go for mediocrity.
- [ ] Managing yourself — achieve control over your work day. Separate the essentials from the inessentials that litter your desk. Know how to simplify your workload — where appropriate, cut corners.

Personal qualities and behaviour

- [ ] Be enthusiastic and show it.
- [ ] Innovate and create — come up with new ideas and react positively to other people's ideas. Don't sulk if your ideas are not accepted. Try again another way.
- [ ] Show willing — there is nothing worse than the person who always moans when he is given something to do. Don't say: 'How can I possibly do that?' Instead, respond immediately with something like this: 'Right, this is what I propose to do — is that what you want?'
- [ ] Be positive — in the words of the old Bing Crosby song: 'accentuate the positive and eliminate the negative'.
- [ ] Work hard — people who get on are hard workers. But

they don't work for work's sake. Effectiveness is never a function of how late you stay in the office. It's what you do while you are there that counts.

☐ Present yourself well — life is not all about making a good impression but you might as well make sure that your achievements are known and appreciated. And if people are impressed by executives who are decisive, punctual and answer promptly, why not impress them that way? More good than harm will come of it.

☐ Be ambitious — 'A man's reach should exceed his grasp, or what's a heaven for?' (Robert Browning). But don't overdo it. Don't appear to be more concerned about your future status than with present effectiveness.

☐ Be courageous — take calculated risks, believe in what you are doing and stick to your guns.

☐ Be assertive but not aggressive.

☐ Get your points across firmly and succinctly.

☐ Don't talk too much. Never over-commit yourself. Save up what you want to say until the right moment. Keep your powder dry. Don't shoot your mouth off. 'Whereof one cannot speak, thereon one must remain silent' (Wittgenstein).

☐ Learn to cope with stress. You won't avoid it and you have to live with it. If things are coming at you thick and fast try to slow down. Relax. Take a little time off. Give yourself a chance to put things in perspective.

☐ If things go wrong, bounce back. Accept reverses calmly. Think about what you need to do and then get into action — fast. There is nothing like purposeful activity in these circumstances.

☐ Get people to trust you — you will do this if you never lie or even shade the truth, if you avoid playing politics and if you always deliver what you promise.

☐ Accept constructive criticism.

☐ 'Admit your own mistakes openly, even joyfully' (Townsend). Never make an excuse. Accept the responsibility *and* the blame if you make a mistake.

Chapter 17
Innovating

Innovation is the life-blood of an organization. There is nothing so stultifying to a company — or the people in it — as a belief that the old ways must be the best ways. An organization which tries to stand still will not survive.

Innovation requires a blend of creativity, clear thinking and the ability to get things done. It requires thinkers and doers to work closely together. Top management must create a climate in which managers have the scope to develop new ideas and the resources to implement them.

The success of innovative projects, therefore, can be seen to depend on two things: characteristics of the individual manager and the climate of the organization.

Individual characteristics

To be an effective innovator you need:

- [ ] To have a clear initial view of the results you want to achieve — you should not worry too much to begin with about the ways of achieving them.
- [ ] To define clearly the aims and benefits of the project.
- [ ] To argue the case for the project persuasively.
- [ ] To get support not only from your boss but also from your colleagues and subordinates — you need to build a coalition in which everyone shares equally in the belief that the project is worthwhile.
- [ ] Courage — to take calculated risks and to weather the storm when the inevitable setbacks occur.
- [ ] To be good at getting people into action — to mobilize people to contribute fully to the project means using a participative management style.
- [ ] Power to mobilize support and resources and to get things

104

done.
- The ability to handle interference or opposition to the project — resistance can be open, but it often takes a passive or covert form: criticism of the plan's details, foot-dragging, late responses to requests, or arguments over allocation of time and resources among projects. Covert resistance can be the most dangerous.
- The force of character to maintain momentum, especially after the initial enthusiasm for the project has waned and the team is involved in more tedious work.

Organizational characteristics

The organizational characteristics which encourage innovation are:

- A free flow of information which allows executives to find ideas in unexpected places and pushes them to combine fragments of information
- Close and frequent contact between departments, and an emphasis on lateral as well as vertical relationships providing resources, information and support
- A tradition of working in teams and sharing credit
- Senior executives who believe in innovation and will make the necessary resources available
- Managers with the ability and desire to seize opportunities and to make time available for innovation.

Case studies

Float glass

The development at Pilkington's is sometimes described as a one-man campaign by Alistair Pilkington. This is not entirely correct. Alistair Pilkington did indeed have and deploy the qualities of a successful innovator. He knew what he wanted, he knew it was worthwhile and he was quite ruthless in getting his own way against opposition. But he had the advantage of working in a company where the climate was conducive to innovation. One of the most impressive research establishments in the world was there to provide the skills and facilities required for the enormous development programme. And, of equal importance, was the tradition at Pilkingtons of management by committee. Often considered to act as a brake on innovation and achievement, the committee system did in fact work well for research and development. Because all relevant departments were represented — research, development, production and sales — the float glass project was a fully integrated affair from the very beginning. The problems of cooperation and the misunderstandings that are inevitable in any major new project did not get a chance to flare up. The traditional rivalries between research, development and production did not, of course, vanish overnight. But the will and the machinery were there to minimize tension. And the project was a triumph.

Innovation in management development

John Raimes was personnel manager in the Filton division of the British Aircraft Corporation. He successfully introduced project and do-it-yourself training a dozen years before various management development pundits announced this approach as a major new discovery.

Raimes was dissatisfied with the traditional type of management training course. He believed that managers would get much more out of being involved in a project which dealt with a real issue of immediate concern to the company. If the right group of managers were brought together they could benefit the company with their ideas as well as learning from and about each other, extending their understanding of how a firm is managed and testing their ability to analyse problems and think through new ideas. A do-it-yourself element could be introduced by giving the managers taking part in a project the scope to attend courses, call for outside advice (within limits) and extend their reading on the subject.

Raimes had to sell his idea to top management. He had to exercise all his considerable powers of persuasion to convince them that his concept would be much more beneficial to the company and its managers than conventional training. He had no proof that this would be the case. He could only carry his point by demonstrating his total conviction that he was right. Which he did.

Raimes' own belief in what he was doing was the main reason why he succeeded. But he was helped by the climate in the firm which, as part of the aerospace industry, lived by innovation and creativity. There were people on the board who recognized that the needs of management in this type of industry were different and had to be catered for in an original way.

Chapter 18

Integration

An organization will only function effectively as a system of coordinated activities if the groups of people within it are able to cooperate effectively. They will not necessarily do this unless you consciously work at improving the integration of their activities.

Vertical and horizontal integration

Integration needs to take place both vertically and horizontally. Douglas McGregor said of vertical integration:

> The outstanding fact about relationships in the modern industrial organization is that they involve a high degree of interdependence. Not only are subordinates dependent upon those above them in the organization for satisfying their needs and achieving their goals, but managers at every level are dependent upon all those below them for achieving both their own and organizational goals.

The achievement of satisfactory vertical integration is largely a matter of the way in which people are managed. It is not so much a structural affair, although integration will be more difficult if there are too many layers of management or if spans of control are too wide.

Problems arise because vertical integration is largely dependent on management style. The quality of managers as leaders and motivators varies considerably. It is the bad and indifferent ones who inhibit vertical integration (see Chapter 20).

Horizontal integration needs to take place between different functions or organizational units. It is not just a matter of coordinating activities; it is much more concerned with getting people to work well together. Problems arise because people tend to be more aware of the need to be independent rather than recognizing the importance of interdependence. This applies particularly to relationships between line departments such as production, and staff, or functional departments, such as finance.

Improved horizontal integration has to be worked for, and there is a choice of methods you can use to achieve it. The main ones are listed below:

- ☐ *Coordination.* This is the traditional method. Managers coordinate different units or people carrying out related activities. It should work but often does not, either because the span of control is inappropriate or because people will not necessarily work well together simply because they are told to.
- ☐ *Structural integration.* Group activities by product or customer, so that people can easily relate their tasks to a common objective, rather than by process, where work is more likely to be seen as an end in itself.
- ☐ *Voluntary integration.* Encourage people to communicate with each other and to integrate their activities without reference to higher authority, except where a decision is needed to resolve differences of opinion.
- ☐ *Meetings.* Set up meetings or committees to deal with planning and operational matters requiring integration. To avoid the dangers inherent in 'management by committee' you should ensure that meetings concentrate on resolving policy issues where joint decisions are required rather than attempting to usurp the normal role of management.
- ☐ *Project teams.* Set up teams or working parties to deal with specific issues or problems outside the normal routine; for example, product development, quality control and systems development. Getting people from different departments to work together is a good way of increasing understanding and developing a sense of common purpose.
- ☐ *Communications.* Improve the quality of communications throughout the organization. This is partly a matter of attitude (there has to be the will to communicate and to listen to communications), partly a matter of structure (too many levels of management or too many separate units or departments will inhibit communications), and partly a matter of the systems and techniques used (the more effective use of the spoken or written word). All this is easier said than done. You cannot force people to communicate; you can only encourage them and try to remove barriers of misunderstanding.

☐ *Training.* Training can help to make people more aware of the need to integrate and can improve techniques (communications and getting the most out of meetings). Courses attended by members of different departments can increase understanding. Team-building training, which concentrates on helping people to work better together in groups, can help.

☐ *Understanding of roles.* Help interrelated functions, units and individuals to be aware of their respective roles. This can be achieved by various informal means, as mentioned above. You can also produce more formal definitions and circulate them to all concerned, but this seldom works: it is just possible that the missives will be read by the recipients, but it is most unlikely that they will take any notice of impersonal exhortations. Management by exhortation is the last refuge of the incompetent manager.

☐ *Planning.* Set up planning procedures which involve people in different units and at different levels in jointly formulating policies and preparing plans.

☐ *Management information.* Install management information systems which help to identify areas where joint action is required.

A case study

Two professional institutions had merged, one of which had two sections and the other three, catering for different branches of the profession. The new institution therefore had five sections each anxious to promote its own interests.

The governing body of the institution, the council, was well aware of the fact that while the members of each section recognized that there were financial advantages in being formed into one body, they did not want to lose any of their independence or separate identity.

But there were a number of areas, such as relationships with the government, professional ethics, public image and educational standards where the institution had to present a cohesive front even if the various sections differed in their views about the subject. An integrated approach was therefore required to reconcile the conflicting aims of unity and independence. Unrest and dissent were already in evidence and had to be stopped.

The obvious solution was to integrate activities through the elaborate committee structure of the institution. Overall, there was a general council dealing with policy matters while each sector had its own council which concerned itself with policy issues specific to that sector.

To integrate the many forms of educational activities of which the institution was rightly proud, a general education committee was set up under the general council. Each sector had its own education committee which sent representatives to the general committee. Similar patterns were evolved for other key areas.

But this solution did not work. The sector committees continued to go their own way, ignoring the need to integrate their activities with those of the other sectors. The central specialist committees were emasculated because the sector representatives were not interested in agreeing or even discussing policies which in any way impinged on sectional interests. The general council was not aware of what the sectors were up to in a number of areas and felt it was in danger of losing control.

Other methods of integration had to be attempted. First, extensive discussions led by senior council members took place at all levels to get sector members to recognize the value to them of having a strong united institute to represent their interests. Next, a working party was formed to conduct a detailed analysis of each of the main policy areas to determine which decisions could be made at sectional or council level. Finally, the working party devised a system of strategic planning which started at sector level and, for those issues which were of general interest, proceeded to council level. The planning procedure was devised on an iterative basis, ie initial ideas were floated at sector level and, if they affected the institution as a whole, were then discussed at the appropriate central committee. If there was any dissent the issue was referred back to the sector committee for further discussion before being reconsidered at the centre. To coordinate this whole process for the general council a planning committee was set up to review and integrate plans for each area for submission to the council for its final decision.

The advantage of the approach was not so much the planning procedure itself which did prove to be somewhat elaborate. The great benefit was that issues of general interest were discussed at all levels. No decisions were made about the future of the institution without attention being given to the views of each sector. The council was in a position to pronounce authoritatively on matters of overall concern, in the knowledge that the sector had been given every opportunity to participate in the formulation of the policies of the institution. A sense of common purpose was therefore developed which provided a firm basis for the integration of the institutional activities.

Chapter 19
Interviewing

Everyone believes that he is a good interviewer. Like everyone believes he is a good driver. But bad drivers abound, as road accident statistics prove. And the record of job failures in most organizations can often be attributed to poor selection in the first place. Many research studies have shown that predictions made at interviews often fail because of bias, failure to get the information required, or inability to interpret the information. To minimize these problems you need to adopt a systematic approach, based on a job description and a specification of the sort of person you need to fill the job. You then need to consider the method of interviewing you use, how to conduct the interview and how to evaluate the results.

Approach to the interview

An interview has been described as a conversation with a purpose. It is a conversation in which the candidate should be drawn out to talk freely about himself and his career. Apart from the time when he is talking about the job and the company, the interviewer should restrict himself to asking questions and making encouraging grunts. Open-ended questions will produce the most informative answers; 'yes or no' questions should be avoided as far as possible. If you simply say 'tell me about your present job' you will get most of what you want to know. Gaps can be filled in by asking follow-up questions. Avoid leading questions which indicate the answer you are expecting.

The interview's principal purpose is to provide evidence upon which a prediction can be made of a candidate's suitability for the job. It does, however, have two other aims: to provide the candidate with information about the job and the company, and to give him a favourable impression of the company. This

112

should encourage the good candidate to join and should leave the rejected candidate without any ill-feelings.

Conducting the interview

The interview must be planned to elicit information from the candidate which will enable his experience, qualifications and personal qualities to be measured against the requirements set out in the job specification. There is no one best way of sequencing an interview. A fairly typical approach would be:

1. Put the candidate at his ease — he will be nervous and you want him to relax so that he will express himself freely.
2. Explain how you are going to handle the interview.
3. Start with a brief description of the job and the company. Do not spend too long over this, especially if the candidate is a marginal one. You can elaborate at the end of the interview.
4. Use a biographical approach, inviting the candidate to describe in his own words his education and career to date. Do not delve too deeply into the distant past — spend most time on the current job. Probe if necessary to ensure that the candidate is giving you the full picture. He will naturally try to gloss over any less successful episodes in his career. Get him to tell you not only what he did but why he did it. This is particularly relevant when discussing choice of career and reasons for leaving jobs. It will give you a chance to assess how well he is motivated.
5. Give him the opportunity to talk about his achievements and to explain any setbacks.
6. Allow time at the end of the interview for him to ask questions.

The information gathering part of the interview should last between 20 and 40 minutes, depending on the level of the job.

For key jobs, a second interview by a more senior person is desirable.

Evaluating the interview

The only questions you need to answer at the end of the interview are:

☐ Does this candidate measure up to the job?
☐ How does this candidate compare with other candidates?

Qualifications are relatively easy to assess unless they have been obtained from some obscure institution. Experience should not be too difficult to evaluate once you have taken steps to assure yourself that the candidate has really done what he claims. Job titles are misleading; you must have information on the actual level of responsibility and compare this with what he will be expected to do in each of the key areas of the job for which he is being considered. Information on specific tasks and achievements is helpful.

His progress to date will give you some indication of how he will perform in the future. A steady progression in line with his ambitions is obviously what you are looking for. Anyone can fail once for reasons which are not particularly blameworthy. A pattern of failure, characterized by short stays in jobs, is highly suspect. If any gaps in the candidate's career emerge, find out where he was and what he was doing.

A candidate's personal qualities are difficult to assess at an interview. You may be able to decide quickly whether you like his manner or not, but it is much harder to assess qualities such as drive, ability to work with others and leadership.

Interviewers are always warned about the 'halo effect' which means allowing a favourable impression of, for instance, a candidate's appearance or manner to override judgement on other aspects of his character and ability. Equally dangerous is the 'horns effect' by which too much attention is paid to one unattractive feature. A balanced view must be achieved, which means looking at all aspects of the candidate's career as well as the initial impression he makes, even though this may be a very important part of the job itself.

Information on personality strengths and weaknesses can be obtained by analysing the applicant's career and interests. Someone with high aspirations who has consistently achieved what he set out to do is clearly well motivated. Someone from a poor background who has triumphed over early setbacks has obviously more drive than someone who has not made the most of the opportunities given to him. The candidate's interests may indicate the extent to which he likes mixing with people and taking up leadership positions. An indication of a person's drive and determination can be seen by how energetically he pursues his spare-time activities. Stamp collecting may sound pretty pedestrian, but if the candidate reveals that by sheer application he has become the leading authority in Britain on colonial stamps in the mid-nineteenth century, this will tell you about his ability to achieve something.

Candidates can make revealing statements about themselves if you allow them to talk — they may indeed talk themselves out of a job. If, for example, someone says that he left his last three jobs because his boss didn't appreciate him, this suggests an inability to get on with superiors or a tendency towards paranoia or both. He has drawn attention to a pattern which could well be repeated.

The final assessment

The evidence required to make an assessment of the candidate comes from various aspects of the interview and from the letter of application or application form. It needs to be looked at against the specification and summarized on an assessment form, especially if there are a number of candidates.

Do's and Don'ts of interviewing

DO	DON'T
Plan the interview	Start the interview unprepared
Establish an easy and informal relationship	Plunge too quickly into demanding questions
Encourage the candidate to talk	Ask leading questions
Cover the ground as planned	Jump to conclusions on inadequate evidence
Probe as necessary	
Analyse career and interests to reveal strengths, weaknesses and patterns of behaviour	Pay too much attention to isolated strengths or weaknesses
Maintain control over the direction and time taken by the interview	Allow the candidate to gloss over important facts
	Talk too much

Chapter 20
Leadership

> The word leadership has fallen into disrepute in recent years. But we are now in danger of over-compensating, of accepting the rival heresy that success in industry can be achieved not by leadership at all, but by management science without a man of courage and vision and experience at the head of the enterprise to tell the management scientists what to study and for what purpose (Antony Jay).

Participation, industrial democracy, group dynamics, joint consultation and so on are all very well, but someone has to point the way and that same person has to ensure that everyone concerned gets there. Organizational effectiveness depends on the quality of leadership. There are no substitutes.

Robert Graves' commanding officer in World War One said: 'Men will follow this young officer, if only to see where he is going.' Charismatic leadership of the kind which makes followers go through hell just because they are inspired by their leader is one approach. It can work well in wartime and during crises. But it is not the only way.

Leadership is a function of the law of the situation. As Mary Parker Follett said: 'In the social situation two processes always go together: the adjustment of man and man, and the adjustment of man and the situation.' Churchill made a good wartime leader because the situation demanded a man with his charisma. But he failed as a peacetime prime minister. Attlee, however, his immediate successor, would have made an uninspiring wartime leader but was a most effective prime minister in peacetime when the situation required a cool, analytical approach and the ability to control as diverse a bunch of prima donnas as has ever been assembled in one cabinet.

The sort of personality you have will obviously influence the sort of leader you are. But the best leaders are those who develop the ability to analyse the situation in which they operate — and this means themselves, the people to be led and the task to be carried out. Such an ability is based on an under-standing of:

☐ The role of the leader
☐ What makes a good leader
☐ The factors affecting leadership
☐ The two main functions carried out by leaders — getting the job done and maintaining relationships.

The role of the leader

All managers are by definition leaders in the sense that they can only achieve their objectives with the support of their team, who must be inspired or persuaded to follow them.

Leadership can be defined as the process of encouraging and inspiring individuals and teams to give their best. As a leader, you exist for one reason only: to achieve your task with the help of your group. To do this you must:

☐ Gain the commitment and cooperation of your team
☐ Get your group into action to meet agreed objectives
☐ Make the best use of the skills, talents and energies of each individual in your team.

Your primary role as a leader is to achieve the task by planning, organizing, coordinating, policy making, giving clear instructions, making decisions and monitoring performance.

Your secondary role is to maintain good relationships between yourself and the group and within the group.

What makes a good leader?

The charismatic leader — the man or woman who, by a combination of inspiration, character and drive can persuade their followers to go anywhere — is born not made, although such a leader still has to work hard at making the best use of inherent gifts.

Other leaders are able to get results without being particularly charismatic. They exercise skills which they have learned over the years — by observation, practice and by studying the art of leadership. These skills include analytical ability as well as the ability to communicate and inspire. There is no one right way of leading, and there are no characteristics which guarantee that someone will be an effective leader.

The factors affecting leadership

The four factors you have to take into account in any situation are:

- ☐ The task you have to carry out and the environment in which it has to be achieved
- ☐ The group you have working for you — the way in which they cooperate with one another
- ☐ The individuals in the group — their skills, needs and aspirations
- ☐ Yourself — your leadership skills, the style of leadership you are most comfortable with, and your ability to adapt that style in different circumstances.

Leadership functions

A leader has two main functions: getting the job done and developing good relationships.

To get the job done you should ensure that your team and each individual in it knows:

- ☐ Where they are going — tasks, programmes, targets and standards of performance are clearly defined
- ☐ How they are going to get there — plans for achieving objectives are communicated and agreed
- ☐ Their authority to make decisions
- ☐ The degree of control that will be exercised over them
- ☐ The rewards and punishments that will be used if standards and targets are not achieved.

To develop good relationships you should:

1. Find time to listen to subordinates
2. Be friendly and approachable, although you must maintain sufficient distance from your group to use your authority when necessary
3. Treat members of your team as equals, but without losing the capacity to exert authority when necessary
4. Pay attention to the needs of the individuals in the group, in particular their need to feel a sense of personal achievement in their work, to receive adequate recognition for their achievements, to feel that the job itself is challenging, and to know that they are advancing in experience and knowledge

118

5. Pay attention to the needs of the group by involving people in agreeing objectives and reviewing results, encouraging them to participate in problem solving, building up unity, and ensuring that communications flow freely.

Case studies

Aircrew captains

A study was carried out by Halpin and Winer on the characteristics that made bomber crew captains good leaders. They first asked the crews to describe how their captains exercised their leadership skills. They then asked the crews and the superior officers to assess the captains' capacities as leaders.

In classifying the descriptions given by the crews of their leaders' behaviour, Halpin and Winer, defined two critical factors:

☐ Initiating structure — organizing and defining the task and the relationships between the captain and the crew
☐ Consideration — behaviour indicative of friendship, trust, respect and warmth in relationships between captain and crew.

Typical actions on the part of a good captain in initiating structure include making his attitudes clear to his crew, ruling with an iron hand, maintaining definite standards of performance and making sure that his part in the crew is understood by members.

Typical actions under the heading of consideration include finding time to listen to crew members, looking after the welfare of individual crew members, treating crew members as his equals and being friendly and approachable.

The most interesting point emerging from the analysis of assessments was that in general, commanding officers thought that the most effective captains were strongest on initiating structure, while the crew members thought that the best captains were equally strong on initiating structure and consideration.

John Adair's analysis of leadership

John Adair based his analysis of leadership on a study of the qualities that made Sandhurst officer cadets good or indifferent leaders (he was an instructor there); he then extended his analysis to leaders in all spheres of life — business, the public sector, politics and the armed services.

He referred to the case of a company which switched foremen between different teams of workers. Those foremen who had been assessed as above average by one team were still considered effective by their new group after four months. But those considered below average by their original team were still felt to be poor by their new team. The less effective foremen showed strong hostility towards management for making the switch.

While this case confirmed that there are factors which distinguish good leaders from poor ones, it was still necessary to analyse in greater depth what these factors are — what makes a good 'action-centred leader'.

Adair refuted any attempt to analyse good leaders in terms of their personal qualities. He quoted a survey of 75 top executives which listed several important qualities — judgement, initiative, integrity, foresight, energy, drive, human relations skills, decisiveness, dependability, objectivity, cooperation. However, the identification of these qualities proved a stumbling block, since there are so many different concepts of what each one means. Also, there are many good leaders who lack some of these qualities, and many poor leaders who possess most of them. This sort of analysis does not take us very far.

Adair therefore suggested that a leader should be described in terms of his functions, which he categorized as:

☐ *The task* — to get things done
☐ *The group* — to hold it together and to develop team spirit
☐ *The individual* — to meet the relevant needs of individuals in the group.

These are interdependent: satisfying task needs will also satisfy group and individual needs. Task needs, however, cannot be satisfied unless attention is paid to group and individual needs. And looking after group needs will contribute to satisfying individual needs and vice versa.

The best leaders are those who keep these three needs satisfied and in balance according to the requirements of the situation.

Chapter 21

Management style

The way in which you behave as a manager will, to a degree, be determined by your personality. If you are a natural extrovert whose catching enthusiasm can inspire the people around you, then your style will be basically charismatic. If, on the other hand, you are a quiet sort of person, who believes in a cool assessment of the situation and an appeal to the intellect rather than to the emotions, then you may deploy a much more laid-back, analytical style. Either of these styles – or a mix of them – can be effective. One is not better than another.

But, whatever your personality, you have a choice of approach which depends upon the situation. The different approaches you can use are described below.

Basic management styles

The basic management styles are:

□ *Autocratic* – using your authority to compel people to do what they are told
□ *Democratic* – encouraging people to participate and involve themselves in decision making.

Autocratic sounds hard, but it is not necessarily so. You sometimes have to *tell* people what to do if you want things done: no argument.

On the other hand, democratic may sound soft. Again, this is not necessarily so. There are times when people will be more committed to doing something if they know why they are doing it and feel that they have taken part in putting it together. It's a way of reconciling their own needs and those of the organization.

Neither style is good or bad. As a leader you should be prepared to adjust your approach according to your analysis of the situation: the task, the constraints within which you are working, the individuals you deal with and the group you lead. You should adopt the same approach in similar circumstances. As the occasion demands, you can:

- □ *Tell.* Decide what to do and tell the individual or the group to do it.
- □ *Sell.* Decide what to do but explain why it has to be done.
- □ *Test.* Decide the lines along which you want to act, but before committing yourself, seek opinions and, if necessary, modify your decision.
- □ *Consult.* Define the problem, propose alternative courses of action and seek suggestions on the action to be taken before making the final decision.
- □ *Join.* Define the problem and join in the process of working out alternative courses of action before evaluating them and making the final decision.

These styles move from the autocratic to the democratic, although you as the leader always make the final decision.

Continuum of leadership

This concept of choice was well expressed by Tannenbaum and Schmidt in an article in the *Harvard Business Review*. They suggested that there is a continuum or range of possible leadership behaviour (management style) available to a manager. Each type of action is related to the degree of authority used by the boss and to the amount of freedom available to his subordinates in making decisions.

In the diagram 'the actions seen on the left characterize the manager who maintains a high degree of control, while those seen on the extreme right characterize the manager who releases a high degree of control. Neither extreme is absolute: authority and freedom are never without their limitations.'

Tannenbaum and Schmidt emphasize that one style is not necessarily better than another. It all depends on the circumstances. And these circumstances will include a number of factors or forces which a manager should consider in deciding how to manage.

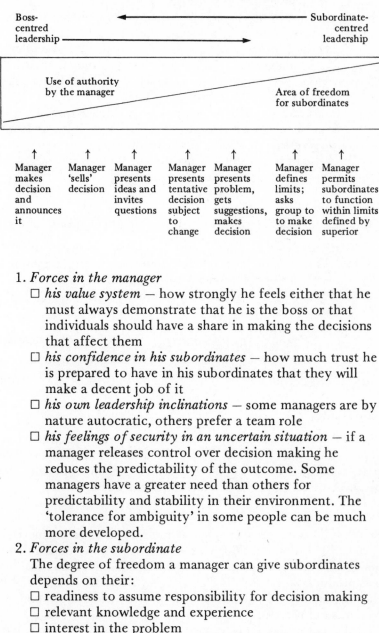

CONTINUUM OF LEADERSHIP BEHAVIOUR

Boss-centred leadership ← → Subordinate-centred leadership

Use of authority by the manager   Area of freedom for subordinates

| Manager makes decision and announces it | Manager 'sells' decision | Manager presents ideas and invites questions | Manager presents tentative decision subject to change | Manager presents problem, gets suggestions, makes decision | Manager defines limits; asks group to make decision | Manager permits subordinates to function within limits defined by superior |

1. *Forces in the manager*
   □ *his value system* — how strongly he feels either that he must always demonstrate that he is the boss or that individuals should have a share in making the decisions that affect them
   □ *his confidence in his subordinates* — how much trust he is prepared to have in his subordinates that they will make a decent job of it
   □ *his own leadership inclinations* — some managers are by nature autocratic, others prefer a team role
   □ *his feelings of security in an uncertain situation* — if a manager releases control over decision making he reduces the predictability of the outcome. Some managers have a greater need than others for predictability and stability in their environment. The 'tolerance for ambiguity' in some people can be much more developed.
2. *Forces in the subordinate*
   The degree of freedom a manager can give subordinates depends on their:
   □ readiness to assume responsibility for decision making
   □ relevant knowledge and experience
   □ interest in the problem
   □ tolerance for ambiguity — many people prefer clear-cut directives, others prefer a wider degree of freedom.

123

3. *Forces in the situation*
   These include:
   □ *the type of organization* — some expect, indeed
     demand, autocratic behaviour, others are more
     permissive; size and complexity influence the situation
   □ *the problem itself* — some decisions can only be made
     by one person, the boss, although he should always ask
     himself the key question 'have I heard the ideas of
     everyone who has the necessary knowledge to make a
     significant contribution to the solution to this problem?'
   □ *the pressure of time* — time pressures may make it
     difficult to consult any people but those who can
     clearly make a contribution to solving the problem.

Conclusions
Tannenbaum and Schmidt came to two significant conclusions:

□ The successful leader is one who is keenly aware of those
  forces which are most relevant to his behaviour at a given
  time. He accurately understands himself, the individuals
  and group he is dealing with, and the company and
  broader social environment in which he operates.
□ The successful leader is one who is able to behave
  appropriately in the light of these perceptions. If direction
  is in order, he is able to direct; if considerable freedom to
  participate is called for, he is able to provide such freedom.

Case studies

The following are descriptions of the management style
deployed by three highly effective managers. In each case the
style was influenced by three factors: the environment, the
people involved, and the personality of the manager.

Edward Smith
Ted Smith was the planning manager in a large engineering
works. He had some 200 people working in the departments
under his control who dealt with process planning, shop loading
and production control. It was a highly responsible job and his
staff included highly qualified engineers as well as large numbers
of clerks doing routine work.

Ted's job was to make sure that his departments ran like
clockwork. Everyone had to know exactly what to do and when
they had to do it. Close cooperation between the three areas

under his control was essential. Charismatic-type leadership was out. He had to be cool, calm, measured and a little bit distant. Everyone in the department had to believe he knew what he was doing and what he wanted.

He therefore held regular meetings with all his subordinates at which he quickly and efficiently reviewed progress, gave instructions and, as and when necessary, discussed problems. At these meetings he was prepared to switch quickly from being someone who knew exactly what he wanted and expected people to do exactly as they were told (because it was sensible and right for them to do so) to someone who was prepared to listen to different views, weigh them up and decide. Sometimes he would deliberately throw his managers a problem and tell them to go away and solve it, and let him know the outcome of their actions.

Ted also ensured that his managers transmitted the content of these meetings down to first line supervisor level. And the latter were encouraged to meet their sections regularly. He emphasized throughout the need for team work and demonstrated his commitment by ensuring that at inter-departmental meetings problems of lack of cooperation or poor communications were given priority. The only time he was ever seen to express anger was when work suffered because of feuds between departments.

Elwyn Jones

Elwyn Jones was the personnel director of a large conglomerate in the food industry with over 80,000 employees. The firm had grown fast by acquisition and was highly decentralized. Staff were deliberately kept to a minimum at headquarters and Jones had only four executives responsible directly to him. He was, however, also responsible for the implementation of group personnel policies in each of the divisions and on these matters the divisional personnel directors were responsible to him.

Jones was not in a position to dictate to divisions what he wanted them to do. He could only influence them, and he felt that he had to get genuine acceptance for new policies before they could be introduced. He therefore had to consult on any changes or innovations he wished to introduce and, in most cases, he had to solicit cooperation on the testing of new ideas.

With his headquarters staff, Jones adopted a highly informal, almost permissive approach. He gave them broad guidelines on how they should develop their ideas in the divisions but encouraged them to think and act for themselves. He never called a formal meeting. He was more likely to withdraw to the local pub where, under the watchful eyes of 'big fat Nellie' behind the bar, he consumed pink gins with his colleagues and discussed strategies on entirely equal terms. He adopted precisely the same approach with the divisional personnel directors, although once or twice a year they all got together in a country hotel (one recommended by the *Good Food Guide*, of course) and spent a pleasant couple of days talking generally about their mutual interests.

James Robinson

Jim Robinson was the managing director of a medium-sized business (1000 employees) in the fast moving consumer goods sector of industry. He had come up the hard way and his experience had always been in similar firms. Business was highly competitive and the pressures on maintaining, never mind increasing, market share were considerable. Tough decisions about products, markets and people had to be made often and quickly. There was a non-executive chairman and three outside non-executive directors on the board, but they let Robinson get on with it as long as he delivered the results they wanted — which he did.

Robinson was a despot, although a benevolent one. He knew much more about the business as a whole than any of the other four executive directors, and the chairman and the key institutions (who were represented by the non-executive directors on the board) relied implicitly on his judgement.

Robinson's management style was rumbustious. He did not suffer fools gladly and he cracked down on any repeated inefficiencies or mistakes. He made the key decisions himself. At meetings of the executive directors he would sometimes say that he wanted the views of those present but stated quite clearly that he had already made up his mind and would need a lot of convincing to change it.

But his deep understanding of the business and his ability to think faster on his feet than anyone else meant that, while his autocratic behaviour was sometimes resented at the time, those subjected to it would say on almost every occasion 'you've got to give it to the old so-and-so — he knows his stuff and he's right'. He led, they followed. This was simply because they knew he could accomplish whatever was required in the volatile environment in which they worked.

Chapter 22
Managing your boss

If you want to achieve results, innovate and get on, you have to learn how to manage your boss. The word 'manage' is defined in the *Oxford English Dictionary* as:

☐ To conduct affairs
☐ To control; cause to submit to one's rule
☐ To bring (a person) to consent to one's wishes by artifice, flattery, or judicious suggestion of motives
☐ To operate upon, manipulate for a purpose
☐ To bring to pass by contrivance; to succeed in accomplishing
☐ To deal with or treat carefully.

Although such concepts as artifice, flattery and manipulation would not normally play any part, all these definitions provide clues as to the various aspects of managing one's boss.

If you really believe that something needs to be done and you cannot do it without the consent of your boss, you have to work out how you are going to manage him. And it is worth careful and continuous thought. It is too easy to neglect this essential part of the art of management.

To manage your boss you need to know how to:

☐ Get agreement from him on what you want to do
☐ Deal with him over problems
☐ Impress him, so that he is more likely to accept your proposals and to place his trust in you.

Getting agreement

Getting agreement from your boss is in many ways like getting agreement from anyone else. You need to be good at case presentation and at persuasion. More specifically you need to do the following things:

1. Find out what he expects
2. Learn about his likes and dislikes, his quirks and his prejudices.
3. Establish how he likes things presented to him. Does he like long, carefully worked out written reports? Or does he prefer a succinct proposal on one side of one sheet of paper? Perhaps he is more likely to be persuaded if he is introduced gradually to a proposal — a softening-up process, as it were. It is often advisable to test the water before plunging straight in. Some people prefer to start by talking all the way round a problem before getting down to its essential elements. They don't like surprises.
4. Get to know how he likes things done — by observation and by asking other people. If something goes wrong, choose the right moment and ask his advice on how to do it better next time (most people love being asked for their advice).
5. Find out the right time to approach him. Some people are at their best first thing. Others take time to warm up. It is obviously inadvisable to spring surprises if he is at the end of a long hard day. Check on his mood in advance. His secretary can help. And it is always worthwhile having her on your side. Secretaries can be good friends but bad enemies.
6. Work out the best circumstances in which to tackle him. Alone in his office, or over lunch, or driving him at speed along a motorway (there is a lot to be said for making him a captive audience). Getting away from the office may be an advantage: there will be no interruptions and your boss is less likely to call in his henchman, and you will not then have to persuade two people at once. (Picking them off one at a time is much more likely to be successful.) Beware of the 'abominable no-man'. Most organizations have at least one — often the head of finance. He no doubt performs a useful role but keep him out of your way if you can.
7. Decide whether you want support. You may be able to make a better case on a one-for-one basis. There is a lot to be said for standing firmly on your own two feet.
8. Don't go in for open confrontation if you cannot get your own way at first. Get your boss to agree with what he is

prepared to agree and then turn to the problem areas.
Impress upon him that you want the two of you to cover
every possible angle. Emphasize joint responsibility.

9. Leave him an escape route — a way open to consent
   without his having to climb down. Don't beat him into the
   ground — you might win this one but what about the next
   time?

10. Don't overwhelm him with your ideas. Don't expect to
    achieve everything at once. Tackle one important thing at
    a time. Keep it simple. If you come up against a strong
    objection don't fight it for too long. Survive to fight
    another day. This does not mean that you should not
    argue your case strongly, but that you should avoid giving
    the impression of being pig-headed.

11. Keep in reserve alternative proposals or modifications to
    your original idea to use if you are getting nowhere.

12. If your boss comes up with a better idea than yours,
    recognize and accept it. Everybody likes recognition.
    There is no need to flatter him. You are only reacting to
    him the way you would like him to react to you.

13. If you can't convince him first time remember that he's
    the boss. He makes the ultimate decisions. If he says 'that's
    the way it's going to be' you *may* have to accept it. In the
    end he could say to you 'we're in a two-horse race and
    only one can win and that's going to be me'. But you don't
    have to give up completely. Watch for any signs that he
    might be prepared to change his mind — given time and a
    revision to your argument or proposal. Don't nag. If you
    press too hard he will become stubborn and begin to think
    that you are challenging his authority and his position.
    Retire in good order and re-open your campaign at the
    right moment.

Dealing with problems

Things are going wrong. You've made a mistake. You need your
boss's help in sorting out a problem. How do you tackle him?
You should adopt the following approach.

1. Keep him informed. Never let him be taken by surprise.
   Prepare him in advance for the bad news. If 'troubles come
   not in single spies but in battalions', don't let him have it
   all at once. Let him down as gently as possible. Don't use

the 'first the good news then the bad news' line too crudely, but don't be too gloomy. Give him hope.

2. If something has gone wrong, explain what has happened, why it has happened (no excuses) and what you would like to do about it. Don't dump the problem in his lap in a 'take it or leave it' spirit.

3. Emphasize that you are seeking his views on what you propose, as well as his agreement.

4. If you think he is to blame, never say 'I told you so'. If you do, you will make an enemy for life.

5. If you admit responsibility, try to stop your boss keeping on at you. Steer him away from recriminations into a positive attitude on what you can *jointly* do to solve the problem.

Impressing your boss

Your purpose as a manager is not solely to impress your boss. Nor is it to make him like you. But you will get more done and get on better if you impress him. And why make an enemy of your boss when you can have him as a friend?

Your boss needs to trust you, to rely upon you and to believe in your capacity to come up with good ideas and to make things happen. He doesn't want to wet-nurse you or to spend his time correcting your mistakes or covering up.

To succeed in impressing your boss without really trying — it's fatal to push too much — you should:

1. Always be frank and open. Admit mistakes. Never lie or even shade the truth. If there is the faintest suspicion that you are not perfectly straightforward, your boss will never trust you again.

2. Aim to help your boss to be right. This does not mean being subservient or time-serving. Recognize, however, that you exist to give him support — in the right direction.

3. Respond fast to his requests on a can do/will do basis.

4. Don't trouble him unnecessarily with your problems.

5. Provide him with protection where required. Loyalty is an old-fashioned virtue, but you owe it to your boss. If you cannot be loyal to him then you should get out from under as quick as you can.

6. Provide your boss with what the army calls 'completed staff work'. This means that if you are asked to do

something you should do it thoroughly. Come up with solutions, not problems. Test your ideas in draft form if you like, but having done so, present a complete proposal with whatever supporting arguments or evidence you need. Avoid half-baked suggestions. Your boss wants answers not questions. When you have finished your report and studied your conclusions and recommendations, ask yourself the question: 'If I were my boss would I stake my reputation on this piece of work and put my name to it?' If the answer is 'No', tear up your report and do it again. It's not completed staff work.

Chapter 23
Meetings

Down with meetings

Meetings bloody meetings, the title of a well-known training film, strikes a familiar chord with us all. When you think how many committees exist and how many meetings are held in any organization, it is remarkable how hard it is to find anyone who has a good word to say for them.

It has been said that committees are made up of the unfit appointed by the incompetent to do the unnecessary, and, again, that a camel is a horse designed by a committee. Experience of badly organized and pointless meetings is so widespread that, for many people, these cynical comments come very close to the truth.

What's wrong with meetings?

Meetings are criticized because they:

- Waste time — too many people talk too much
- Fail to produce decisions and can be slow, exasperating and frustrating — they legitimize procrastination and indecisiveness
- Tend to be dominated by a few people with strong personalities
- Make lowest common denominator recommendations
- Encourage political decisions where vested interests can prevail by means of lobbying and pressure
- Dilute responsibility
- Are costly in time and money
- Concentrate on trivialities they can grasp rather than big issues beyond their scope. Northcote Parkinson cited as an example of this a committee which approved a £1 million capital development project (which it couldn't properly

understand) in ten minutes flat yet spent two hours arguing about a new cycle shed costing £800.

What's right with meetings?

Meetings tend to incite such criticism because they are not properly organized. Many of the criticisms levelled at meetings are really criticisms of their misuse, not their proper use. A well organized meeting held at the right time for the right reasons can bring a number of benefits. It can:

- ☐ Ensure that important matters get proper consideration from all involved
- ☐ Clarify thinking in that members have to justify their positions before the others present
- ☐ Ensure that different viewpoints are aired
- ☐ Act as a medium for the exchange of information
- ☐ Save time by getting a number of people together
- ☐ Promote coordination
- ☐ Create something as a group which the individuals could not have achieved working separately — this is the process of synergy, where the whole is greater than the parts.

To make meetings work there are three things that must happen:

- ☐ They should be set up properly
- ☐ There should be a good chairman
- ☐ The members should be able to participate effectively.

Do's and Don'ts of meetings

DO	DON'T
Use a meeting if the information or the judgement is too great for one man	Use a meeting if one man can do the job better
Set up committees only when it is essential to assemble people with different viewpoints in one place at one time	Set up a committee if you want sharp, clear responsibility
	Use a committee to administrate anything
Appoint a chairman who is going to be able to control the meeting and get the best out of it	Use a meeting or committee if you need speedy action
Put people with different backgrounds on the committee who can contribute ideas	Appoint a bigger committee than you need — over ten people can become unwieldy
Tell committees what they are to do and what their authority is	

DO	DON'T
Tell committees what they are to do and what their authority is	Hold unnecessary meetings — it may be a good thing to meet regularly on the first Friday of every month but it may be an even better thing to meet only when you have something to discuss.
Be explicit about when you want the meeting to report back	
Use meetings where they work best — reviewing or developing policies, coordinating decisions, ensuring that all concerned with a programme are consulted and kept informed	
Wind up committees as soon as they have served their purpose.	

Chairmanship

The success or failure of a meeting largely depends on the chairman. If you are chairing a meeting this is what you must do:

Prior to the meeting
Before the meeting starts ensure that it has proper terms of reference and that the members are briefed on what to expect and what they should be prepared to contribute. Plan the agenda to provide for a structured meeting, covering all the issues in a logical order. Prepare and issue briefing papers which will structure the meeting and spell out the background, thus saving time going into detail or reviewing purely factual information during the meeting.

During the meeting
1. Start by clearly defining the objective of the meeting, setting a time scale which you intend to keep.
2. Go through each item of the agenda in turn ensuring that a firm conclusion is reached and recorded.
3. Initiate the discussion on each item by setting the scene very briefly and asking for contributions — ask for answers to specific questions (which you should have prepared in advance) or you may refer the matter first to a member of the meeting who can make the best initial contribution (ideally you should have briefed that individual in advance).
4. Invite contributions from other members of the meeting, taking care not to allow anyone to dominate the discussions.

5. Bring people back to order if they drift from the point.
6. If there is too much talk, remind members that they are there to make progress.
7. Encourage the expression of different points of view and avoid crushing anyone too obviously if he has not made a sensible comment.
8. Allow disagreement between members of the meeting but step in smartly if the atmosphere becomes too contentious.
9. Chip in with questions or brief comments from time to time, but do not dominate the discussion.
10. At appropriate moments during the meeting summarize the discussion, express views on where the committee has got to and outline your perception of the interim or final decision that has been made. Then check that the meeting agrees, amending the conclusion as necessary, and ensure that the decision is recorded exactly as made.
11. Summarize what has been achieved at the end of the meeting, indicating who has to do what by when.
12. If a further meeting is needed, agree the purpose of the meeting and what has to be done by those present before it takes place.

Members

If you are a member of a meeting you should:

1. Prepare thoroughly — have all the facts at your fingertips, with any supporting data you need.
2. Make your points clearly, succinctly and positively — try to resist the temptation of talking too much.
3. Remain silent if you have nothing to say.
4. Keep your powder dry if you are not leading the discussion or if it is a subject you are not knowledgeable about. Listen, observe and save your arguments until you can make a really telling point. Don't plunge in too quickly or comprehensively — there may be other compelling arguments.
5. If you are not too sure of your ground, avoid making statements such as 'I think we must do this'. Instead, pose a question to the chairman or other member of the meeting such as, 'Do you think there is a case for doing this?'
6. Be prepared to argue your case firmly, but don't persist

in fighting for a lost cause. Don't retire in a sulk because you cannot get your own way; accept defeat gracefully.

7. Remember that if you are defeated in committee, there may still be a chance for you to fight another day in a different setting.

Chapter 24
Motivation

If your staff are going to achieve the results you are aiming at, they must be well motivated. That is, they must be made to want what you want them to want.

Ensuring that your staff are well motivated is essentially a matter of using the leadership skills and appropriate management style discussed in earlier chapters. An understanding of the process of motivation will greatly enhance your chances of success.

What is motivation?

Motivation is what makes people act or behave in the way they do. When we observe people behaving in a certain way, we ask: 'What are their motives?' If we want them to do something, we ask: 'How can we motivate them?'

Motivation and needs

Motivation begins with the needs that exist within us all. If these are unsatisfied we establish a goal, consciously or unconsciously, and take action to achieve that goal. The basic motivation model therefore looks like this:

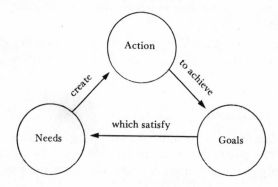

Most people make the mistake of trying to motivate others on the basis of faulty assumptions about their future behaviour. People's needs and the ways in which they are satisfied are much more complex than we tend to think. We observe behaviour and draw conclusions from it, but very often we do not really know what the motivating factor is.

The following is an example of how a superficial analysis of needs can lead a company astray:

> The management of an aircraft assembly plant in the UK fell into this trap a few years ago when they were in the happy position of having a full order book and a shortage of skilled craftsmen. To achieve production deadlines, they recruited fitters from all parts of the country, promising help with settling-in costs and removal expenses. Unfortunately, a very high proportion of the fitters (nearly 50 per cent) left within three months when they were just beginning to become effective. Heavy recruitment costs had to be written off and production suffered.
>
> The immediate reaction of the factory manager was that the newly engaged fitters needed more money. He could not alter basic rates but he encouraged his rate fixers to relax times and so increase bonus earnings. But labour turnover carried on at the same high rate, although earnings were increased all round.
>
> The factory manager therefore asked the personnel manager to investigate the problem more thoroughly. The latter interviewed every fitter who was leaving and also a large sample of existing workers. He got the same story from everybody. Because this was the first production run there were many modifications and design changes. This led to shortages of tools and parts. The fitters felt they were being messed about and were utterly frustrated by the constant interruptions and delays. Moreover, their earnings fluctuated considerably. They never knew what was going into their pay packets from one week to the next and this caused great difficulties with their wives, who were trying to adjust to new surroundings and expenditures.
>
> Hardly any of the fitters complained about the level of earnings, it was their unpredictability that concerned them. Their basic needs were for a settled working environment and an end to wildly fluctuating pay packets, not extra cash.

To avoid this sort of problem you need to know more about the needs affecting motivation — how they are classified and how they operate.

Classification of needs

The most famous classification of needs is the one formulated by Maslow. He suggested that there are five major need categories which apply to people in general, starting from the fundamental physiological needs and leading through a hierarchy of safety, social and esteem needs to the need for self-fulfilment, the highest need of all.

Another behavioural scientist, Frederick Herzberg, developed what he called a two factor model of human needs at work, on the basis of what some people regard as rather spurious research. One group of factors revolves around the need for people to develop in their job as a source of personal growth — it includes the needs for achievement, responsibility and recognition. The second group is associated with the needs for fair treatment in pay, supervision, working conditions and administrative practices.

How needs operate
According to Maslow, man is a wanting animal. It is unsatisfied needs that drive him forward. As one need is satisfied, the next one in the hierarchy emerges.

Herzberg looked at needs another way. He suggested that his first group of needs — those associated with the work itself: responsibility, achievement etc — are the real satisfiers because they seem to be effective in motivating the individual to superior performance and effort. The second group of needs — those associated with the environment in which work is carried out: pay, conditions etc — serve primarily to prevent job dissatisfaction, while having little effect on positive job attitudes. Herzberg christened this second group the 'hygiene' factors.

Herzberg and many others who have followed him thus distinguished between the *intrinsic* factors arising from the work itself, and the *extrinsic* factors provided by the employer, such as pay. The claim has been made that while extrinsic rewards can be important in increasing effort and minimizing dissatisfaction, intrinsic rewards relating to responsibility and achievement may have a longer and deeper effect in creating and increasing job satisfaction. The whole creed of 'job enrichment' (giving people more responsibility and scope in their jobs) has been founded on this belief.

While classifications of needs may be helpful, their use in understanding the complex nature of motivation is limited. For instance, even Herzberg had to admit that money 'takes on some of the properties of a motivator with dynamics similar to recognition for achievement', and neither he nor anyone else has been able to prove a significant relationship between satisfaction of needs and performance. We therefore need to look at other aspects of motivation.

The relationship between satisfaction and performance

It is clearly simplistic to believe that a happy worker is a productive worker. There are some people who are quite happy to do nothing. But it could be equally simplistic to think that a satisfied worker is *necessarily* a productive worker. There is such a thing as being self-satisfied. Moreover, the numerous research projects on motivation carried out within factories and offices over the last fifty years have failed to produce convincing evidence that satisfaction leads to good performance. It has been shown that satisfaction explains less than 20 per cent of variances in performance. Indeed, it is possible to say that it is not satisfaction that produces good performance, but good performance that produces satisfaction.

We must therefore reject the theory that passive and historical feelings of job satisfaction are the key motivators — an essentially static theory — and look at the more dynamic aspects of motivation in the shape of what people are seeking in the future — their expectations.

The role of expectations

Motivation is a forward-looking process. The degree to which we are motivated depends very much on our perception of the likelihood that certain behaviour will achieve the results we want. Motivation is much more about expectations than about satisfactions. This concept of expectancy was formulated by Vroom, among others. He wrote:

> Whenever an individual chooses between alternatives which involve certain outcomes, it seems clear that his behaviour is affected not only by his preference among these outcomes but also by the degree to which he believes these outcomes to be probable .... An expectancy is defined as a momentary belief that a particular act will be followed by a particular outcome.

Thus, in the case of the aircraft company mentioned earlier, the fitters were de-motivated because their expectations about a steady flow of earnings were disappointed, not because they were not enough.

It follows from this commonsense proposition — people will only be motivated if they think they are going to get what they want (or avoid what they don't want) — that expectations about rewards have an important impact on motivation. We must therefore consider the role of the reward system.

The reward system

It was suggested above that good performance causes satisfaction — a sense of achievement. And Douglas McGregor said that: 'Commitment to objectives is a function of the rewards associated with their achievement.'

If we want effort from the people who work for us there are two factors we must consider:

☐ The value of the rewards to the individual in so far as they are likely to satisfy his needs for security, social esteem, and self-fulfilment,

☐ The probability that rewards depend on effort, as perceived by the individual; in other words, his expectations about the relationship between his effort and his reward.

Thus, the greater the value of a set of rewards and the higher the probability that receiving each of these rewards depends upon effort, the greater the effort that will be made in a given situation.

The painstaking research of countless behavioural scientists seems therefore to have resulted in the 'discovery' that effort depends on the rewards people can expect to get — a fact which any sensible line manager knows without resort to research. But effort is not enough. It has to be effective effort if it is to produce what we want. And there are a number of additional factors which affect motivation.

Other factors affecting motivation

☐ *Ability* — the individual's intelligence, skills and know-how.

☐ *Perceptions about the job* — what the individual wants to do or thinks he is required to do. From the organization's point of view, it is desirable that the individual's perceptions should coincide with what it believes he ought to be doing.

☐ *Influence of other people* — the pressures exerted on a person by fellow employees, family and other social groups to which they belong. Group pressures are

141

important because they affect social needs and the need for esteem.

☐ *The work itself* – the extent to which the work itself gives people an opportunity for achievement, responsibility and satisfaction. The following story is an example of how the quality of working life, resulting from the way jobs are designed, can affect performance.

In the new policies department of an insurance company, output, as measured by policies issued per clerk, was falling badly. A preliminary investigation suggested that high labour turnover was a major causal factor. A further investigation indicated that the nature of the work itself was the problem. The qualification level for new entrants was fairly high – four or more O Levels. But the clerks were put on absolutely routine work. Each one dealt with a single stage in the process of dealing with new insurance policies. Their work was then checked by another section. Some people therefore spent their whole day checking or re-checking other people's work, a soul-destroying occupation. If any interesting work needed to be done it was hived off to a department of specialists. Only routine work went down what was aptly called 'the pipe line'. The answer to the problem was to give each clerk whole segments of work, including the interesting bits. There was a significant reduction in staff turnover and improvement in performance.

These variables affecting performance can be expressed in the model shown below, which is based on the important work of Lawler and Porter in this field:

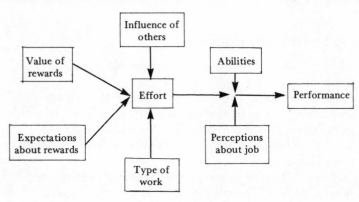

Motivation in practice

The analysis of the process of motivation in this chapter suggests certain things that you can do as a manager to improve your ability to motivate. These are:

1. Try to understand what the needs of your subordinates are in terms of Maslow's categories: security, social, esteem, self-fulfilment.
2. Find out not only what they need but also what they want. You may not be able to give it to them but you might at least be able to modify your approach to motivation in the light of this knowledge.
3. Use financial rewards as a prime motivator. Money is important because it satisfies so many needs — it provides what people want to increase their standard of living, but it also serves as the most effective way of recognizing achievement (self-fulfilment) and enabling people to demonstrate their achievement to others (esteem).
4. Bear in mind, however, that money is not the only reward that people need and want. They can also be motivated by recognition, praise, promotion and the work itself — the opportunity to achieve something extra or to take on greater responsibility. And this sort of reward can sometimes be more effective than money. It depends on their individual needs, and the reason you should try to identify these needs is that you can be more discriminating in the use of rewards.
5. Remember the importance of expectations as an influence on motivation. A reward will be much more effective when people know what they can get if they work hard and well enough. You should therefore:
   - Ensure that the relationship between effort and reward is clearly defined in any financial reward system — payment by results, commission or bonus schemes
   - Set your subordinates targets and standards which are achievable but not too easily
   - Make them aware that their achievements will be recognized by praise, a special reward or the opportunity to do better — but don't cheapen the reward, give praise only when praise is due
   - Make it known, as far as possible, what people have to do to gain promotion or take on greater responsibility
   - Spell out not only what they can get if they do well but

also what they won't get if they do badly. This is not a crude carrot and stick tactic but a clarification of the fact that what they achieve or don't achieve is up to them.

6. Always keep in mind that your aim, as defined by Douglas McGregor, is 'the creation of conditions such that the members of the organization can achieve their own goals *best* by directing their efforts towards the success of the enterprise'. Hence the value of:

   — Identifying people's needs, so that you can try to adjust rewards to meet those needs
   — Getting people to think for themselves about what they can and should do and agreeing targets and standards with them.

7. Recognize the fact that people can be motivated by the work itself if it satisfies their needs for responsibility and achievement. Do this by using the following job enrichment techniques:

   — Increasing the responsibility of individuals (as in the insurance company case mentioned earlier)
   — Giving people more scope to vary the methods, sequence and pace of their work
   — Giving a person or group a complete natural unit of work, thus reducing specialization
   — Removing some controls from above while ensuring that individuals or groups are clearly accountable for achieving defined targets or standards
   — Giving people the control information needed to monitor their own performance
   — Encouraging the participation of employees in planning work and innovating new techniques
   — Assigning projects to individuals or groups which give them more responsibility and help them to increase their expertise.

8. Remember that group pressures can affect motivation, for good or ill. Take steps to get groups on your side by involving them in key decisions which affect their work.

Chapter 25

Negotiation

Negotiation is the process of coming to terms and, in so doing, getting the best deal possible for your firm, your union or yourself.

Negotiations involve a conflict of interest. Sellers prefer a high price to a low one and buyers prefer a low price to a high one. Unions want the highest settlement they can get, management wants the lowest. What one side gains the other loses. No one likes to lose, so there is conflict, which has to be managed if an amicable agreement is to be achieved. And negotiators do, or should, try to end up on friendly terms, whatever differences of opinion have occurred on the way. After all, they may well meet again.

Another important feature of negotiations is that they take place in an atmosphere of uncertainty. Neither side necessarily knows what the other wants or will give.

There are two main types of negotation — commercial and trade union.

Commercial negotiations

Commercial negotiations are mainly about the price and the terms for supplying goods or services.

In their simplest form they are no more than a haggle between buyer and seller, much the same as what happens when you trade in your car for a new one. At their more complex they concern a package in which a number of extras are on offer along with the basic product. Sellers can usually offer a range of prices to suit the needs of the buyer. An 'ex-works' price, a delivered price, an installed price and a price which includes service. Various methods of staging payments or providing credit may also be offered.

Negotiations of this type usually start with the buyer

producing his specification. The seller then produces a proposal and negotiation starts. The seller will have included a negotiating margin in his proposal and will be prepared to vary his price according to the package required.

Commercial negotiations are usually conducted in a friendly manner, and that's your major problem. You can too easily be seduced into accepting a less than satisfactory deal by the blandishments of the negotiator.

Trade union negotiations

Trade union negotiations can be much tougher. They may involve a simple pay settlement, but usually they involve a package. Extra benefits will be at issue, which can be traded for concessions if need be.

In this type of negotiation, both parties are probably quite clear as to the maximum they will give or the minimum they will accept. They will have predetermined their opening demands and offers and their shopping list of extras will have been analysed to determine which points can be conceded in return for some benefit.

There are a number of bargaining conventions used in union negotiations, of which the following are the most generally accepted:

- ☐ Whatever happens during the bargaining, both parties hope to come to a settlement.
- ☐ Attacks, hard words, threats and (controlled) losses of temper are treated by both sides as legitimate tactics and should not be allowed to shake either party's belief in the other's integrity, or their desire to settle without taking drastic action.
- ☐ Off-the-record discussions (beneficial as a means of probing attitudes and intentions) should not be referred to specifically in formal bargaining sessions, unless both sides agree in advance.
- ☐ Each side should be prepared to move from its original position.
- ☐ It is normal, although not inevitable, for the negotiation to proceed by a series of offers and counter-offers which lead steadily towards a settlement.
- ☐ Concessions, once made, cannot be withdrawn.
- ☐ Firm offers must not be withdrawn, although it is

legitimate to make and withdraw conditional offers.
- ☐ A third party should not be brought in until both parties are agreed that no further progress would be made without one.
- ☐ The final agreement should mean exactly what it says. There should be no trickery and the terms agreed should be implemented without amendment.
- ☐ If possible, the final settlement should be framed so that both sides can save face and credibility.

The process of negotiation

In both cases the process is much the same. Here each stage is illustrated by a summary of what took place in an actual trade union negotiation.

Stage 1: Preparation — Setting objectives (or drawing up specifications) assembling data, and deciding on negotiating strategy

The union's aim was to achieve a settlement at, or above, the current rate of inflation (8 per cent). Its strategy was to force management on to the defensive by asking them to make an offer without divulging what the union wanted. In addition, the union asked for a reduction of one hour in the working week, an extra three days' holiday and a Christmas bonus of one week's pay.

The management's objective was to settle at no more than the rate of inflation, and to concede nothing that would raise the total cost of the package above 8 per cent. There was some debate within the management team about strategy. One hawk wanted to pre-empt the union claim by starting with the final offer, allowing no room for bargaining. He was overruled on the grounds that this would cause a confrontation and hence long-term damage to relations with the union. The next question was how much room for manoeuvre should be allowed between the opening and closing offer. Some wanted to start as low as possible, say 3 per cent, so as to close well below the 15 per cent claim expected from the union. The prevailing view, however, was that too low an offer would prolong the negotiations unnecessarily. It was thought better to start at 5 per cent, so that, if it had to, the firm could take two steps of 1½ per cent before reaching its maximum of 8 per cent.

Stage 2: Opening — Negotiators reveal their initial bargaining positions to their opposite numbers

The union started by stating its case. It wanted a substantial increase to protect its members from inflation and to restore the differentials lost over the previous three years. The extras (reduced working week, etc) were thrown in almost as make-weights, giving management the clue that there might be scope for some trading later on.

Management stated that no 'substantial offer' could be expected. It emphasized the poor trading results of the firm and the fact that overall, the pay of the union's members compared favourably with other workers. The point was also made (it was to be repeated many times in ensuing meetings) that the firm could not guarantee that pay increases would match inflation. Having set out their opening positions and their main arguments the two parties agreed to adjourn the meeting.

Stage 3: Bargaining — At this stage both parties have the same aims. As a negotiator you will be trying: (a) to probe the weaknesses in the other side's case, and (b) to convince the other side that they must abandon their position and move closer to your own. You will also be checking to see if your own position holds good in the light of information received from your opponents and their reactions to your case. Your original judgement may be confirmed or you may have to adjust it now. You may also decide to apply pressure or give concessions now in order to move towards a satisfactory conclusion.

In the bargaining stage three meetings were held. At each of them the arguments of both management and union teams were the same as in the opening phase.

Each party aimed to discover how strongly the other believed in his arguments and to what extent he was prepared to shift his position. Every phrase was analysed to discover just what was behind it, both sides seeking hints as to how much support the other was getting — from the shop floor and top management respectively.

Management opened with a 5 per cent offer and got the usual reaction: it was 'derisory', 'insulting' and so on. The union refused to state exactly what it wanted, hoping to mystify and wrong-foot the management.

Between the second and third meetings the management team were agreed in the belief that the union was hoping to get 10 per cent but, if pushed, might settle for eight. It was decided that an offer to reduce the working week by 30 minutes might be made, but only as a last-minute trade-off if a reasonable settlement seemed unlikely.

At the third meeting, management increased its offer to 7 per cent, saying that this was as far as it could go. When pressed to state whether this was, or was not, their final offer, the management team refused to elucidate. The union rightly interpreted this to mean that there was more in the kitty and that top management would release it if pressed hard enough. The union demanded 10 per cent *and* the other concessions.

Stage 4: Closing — Each party judges whether the other side is determined to stick to its position or will settle for a compromise. The final moves are made. It is during this stage that final 'trade-offs' may lead to a settlement.

The final meeting lasted all day and into the night. Management stuck to its 7 per cent offer and made no other concessions. The union tried several tactics. Pleading, controlled loss of temper and threats of industrial action were all used. The management team finally judged that the only way to get a settlement was to attempt a trade-off. They offered 7 per cent plus one hour off the working week, in return for an agreement to abolish the customary five minutes 'wash up' time (a practice that had been consistently abused).

Management reiterated that this was the final offer and was as much as the firm could afford and managed to convince the union by sheer force of argument that it meant what it said. The union accepted the offer after balloting its members.

Negotiating tactics

a. Preparation
1. Define your bargaining objectives as follows:

   □ *Ideal* — the best you can hope to achieve
   □ *Minimum* — the least you would be prepared to settle for
   □ *Target* — what you are going to try for and believe, realistically, you have a good chance of achieving.
2. Consider how you might build up a package which would allow concessions to be exchanged. For example, could you accept a higher price for a concession on payment terms? Or increase a pay offer if the union agrees to remove a restrictive practice.

3. Assess what the other party wants or is prepared to offer. For example, if you are a manufacturer negotiating terms with a store it pays to know, say, that the buyer is constrained by his company policy which insists on a three-times mark up. Knowing the retail price that the store will want to charge you will have a good idea of the maximum the buyer will pay. You can then judge whether you should press for a larger order to justify a lower selling price than you would normally accept.

In a typical wage negotiation the union or representative body making the claim will come to the table with a predetermined target, minimum and opening claims. Similarly, you, as the employer, will have your own target, maximum and opening offer.

The difference between their claim and your offer is the negotiating range. If your maximum exceeds their minimum this will indicate the settlement zone. This is demonstrated in the diagram below.

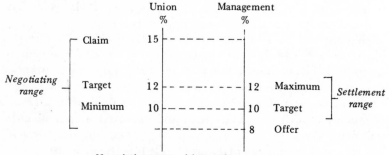

Negotiating range with a settlement zone

In this example the chance of settlement without too much trouble is fairly high. It is when your maximum is less than their minimum, as in the diagram below, that the trouble starts.

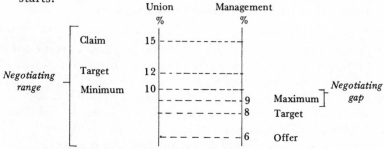

Negotiating range without a settlement zone

4. Decide on your strategy and tactics — your opening offer, the steps you are going to take, the concessions you are prepared to offer and the arguments you are going to use.
5. Collect the facts needed to support your case.
6. Assemble any documents you need, such as standard contract terms.
7. In a trade union negotiation:
   ☐ Select the negotiating team. This should never have fewer than two members, and for major negotiations should have three or more: one to take the lead, one to take notes and feed the negotiator with any supporting information he needs, and the others to observe their opposite numbers and play a specific part in negotiations in accordance with their brief.
   ☐ Brief the members of the negotiating team on their roles and the negotiating strategy and tactics that are to be adopted. If appropriate, prepared statements or arguments should be issued at this stage to be used as required by the strategic plan.
   ☐ Rehearse the members of the team in their roles. They can be asked to repeat their points to other members and deal with responses from them; or someone can act as devil's advocate and force the leader or other members of the team to handle awkward points or negotiating ploys.

At this stage it may be possible to meet the opponent informally to sound out his position, while he sounds out yours. You can use such a session as an 'early warning' system to get your opponent to modify his initial demands by convincing him of the strength of your own position or your determination to resist.

In a recent trade union negotiation these 'corridor tactics' met with success. The union concerned had asked management to introduce a new technology agreement with the usual clauses about consultation, job protection and health precautions.

During the first two meetings management stuck firmly to its view that all these requirements were catered for by existing agreements and published policies. But the union insisted that this was not so. The negotiation seemed to have reached an impasse. Whatever the union leader felt, he could not weaken too obviously during the actual meetings. Neither could the general manager who was heading the management team.

To break the impasse the general manager asked his industrial relations manager to hold an off-the-record meeting with the trade union leader. At this meeting it was made clear that the company would not agree to a separate new technology agreement in any circumstances. But the industrial relations manager suggested that the company would be prepared to add a stronger prior consultation clause to the existing agreement.

From previous experience, the union leader knew this man meant what he said. He saw no point in having a major confrontation on this issue and knew he would get little support from his members, who did not see new technology as a real issue. But he felt that if he had to give a concession he should get something back. In other words, he wanted a trade-off.

He therefore agreed to go along with the idea, so long as the company let the union monitor the introduction of any major new technology schemes over the next six months. This was accepted by the industrial relations manager. Both parties understood the convention that there was no commitment and that no reference would be made to their discussion in future formal meetings. They then cleared the informal understanding with their respective committees and, at the subsequent formal meeting, the terms were agreed without any difficulty. What looked to be a major problem had been solved by corridor negotiations.

b. Opening
Your tactics when opening the negotiation should be to:

- ☐ Open realistically and move moderately
- ☐ Challenge your opponent's position as it stands; but on no account to limit his ability to move
- ☐ Explore attitudes, ask questions, observe behaviour and, above all, listen; assess your opponent's strengths and weaknesses, his tactics and the extent to which he may be bluffing
- ☐ Make no concessions of any kind at this stage
- ☐ Be non-committal about proposals and explanations (do not talk too much).

c. Bargaining
Your aim is to narrow the gap between the two initial positions and to persuade your opponent that your case is so strong that he must accept less than he had planned. You should:

- ☐ Always make conditional proposals: 'If you will do this

I will consider doing that'
- [ ] Never make one-sided concessions: always trade off against a concession from the other party: 'If I concede x then I expect you to concede y'
- [ ] Negotiate on the whole package: never allow your opponent to pick you off item by item; keep all the issues open so as to extract the maximum benefit from potential trade-offs.

READING THE SIGNALS

During the bargaining stage you must be sensitive to any signals made by the other party. Every time he makes a conditional statement it shows that he is prepared to move. Explore the possibilities with questions. Try to get behind what people *say* and understand what they really *mean*. For example:

What they say	What they mean
That's as far as I can go.	I might be able to persuade my boss to go further.
We don't usually give more than 5 per cent discount.	We're prepared to give more if you give us something in return.
Let's think about that point.	I'm prepared to negotiate.
I need notice of that question.	It's difficult, but not impossible. Try again.
It will be very difficult for us to meet that requirement.	It's not impossible but we'll want a trade-off.
I shall certainly consider your offer.	I am going to accept it but I don't want to appear to be too easy a touch.
This is our standard contract.	We're prepared to negotiate on the terms.
We're prepared to offer you £x per 1000 units.	The price is negotiable.
That's my final offer.	My boss *might* go further if pushed (or if it is made worth his while).
We couldn't meet your delivery requirements at that price.	I will negotiate on delivery or price.

ARGUING

During the bargaining stage much of your time will be spent in arguing. Clear thinking (see Chapter 6) will help you to present your case and expose the fallacies in your opponent's arguments.

You should also consider the *manner* in which you argue. You are not there to beat your opponent into the ground. In fact, in the interests of future good relationships (which will benefit *you* as well as him) it is wise to provide him with an

153

escape route. As Victor Feather said: 'Always leave the other fellow the price of his bus ticket home.'

Avoid brow-beating your opponent. Disagree with him firmly, but don't shoot him down. Don't try to make him look small. Score points over him, if you must, to discredit his arguments or expose fallacious reasoning but never in order to discredit him as a person. If you indulge in personal attacks or abuse your opponents will close ranks.

To argue effectively you must be prepared to listen both to the stated, and to the implied points made by your opponent. Don't talk too much yourself, it will prevent you reading signals, and you may give too much away. Wherever you can, challenge your opponent to justify his case on an item-by-item basis. Put the onus on him by questioning for clarification. Answer a question with another question if you want time to consider.

Argue calmly and without emotion, but emphasize the points you really want to ram home either by raising your voice slightly and slowing down to highlight your argument, or by repetition.

Control your anger. Express yourself strongly, by all means, but you will lose everything if you lose your temper.

Always remember that you are *not* trying to win at all costs. If he wants something which you cannot give, don't just say no. Offer an alternative package. If he is asking for a higher specification than you normally provide for the price and wants a delivery date which you cannot meet without incurring extra overtime costs, tell him that you can meet the specifications and the delivery deadline as long as he is prepared to cover the costs.

GAMBITS

There are a number of standard bargaining gambits. Here are a few of the more common ones:

- ☐ *Uttering threats* — 'Agree to what I want or I'll call out the lads'; or '. . . I'll take my custom elsewhere'. Never react to such threats and never utter empty ones.
- ☐ *No negotiation under duress* — 'We refuse to discuss your claim unless and until you cancel your overtime ban.' An excellent approach, if you can get away with it.
- ☐ *It will reflect badly on you* — 'Do you really want to get the reputation of being a heartless employer?' This is an

emotional appeal and, as such, should be discounted.

☐ *The bluff direct* — 'I have two or three quotations lower than yours.' The answer to this gambit is to call his bluff — 'What are they offering for the price?' 'OK why not accept them, why bother talking to me?'

☐ *The leading question* — 'Do you think it is a good idea to reward people according to merit?' 'Yes'. 'Then why do you insist on retaining this fixed incremental scheme which benefits everybody irrespective of how well they've done?' Never fall for a leading question.

☐ *The piecemeal or 'salami' technique* — In this your opponent will try to pick off the items one by one. 'That's the price agreed, now we can deliver in three months, OK?' 'Right, we've agreed the delivery terms, now this is how we charge for maintenance.' Always negotiate the whole package. Don't allow yourself to be railroaded into a piecemeal approach.

☐ *The yes, but . . . — approach* — 'Yes, we agree to accept an increase of 8 per cent but before we can agree to everything there is this other problem of compensation for redundancy we must tackle.' To avoid being caught in a yes/but trap, always make offers on one part of a package conditional on accepting another part: 'We are prepared to consider an 8 per cent offer but only if you agree to drop your claim for enhanced redundancy pay.'

d. Closing

When and how you close depends on your assessment of the strength of your opponent's case and his determination to see it through. You may close by:

1. Making a concession, preferably a minor one, and trading it off against an agreement to settle. The concession can be offered more positively than at the bargaining stage: 'If you will agree to settle at x, I will concede y.'
2. Doing a deal: You might split the difference, or bring in something new — such as extending the settlement time-scale, agreeing to back payments, phasing increases, making a joint declaration of intent to do something in the future (for example to introduce a productivity plan), or offering an incentive discount.
3. Summarizing what has happened to date, emphasizing the concessions that have been made and the extent to which

you have moved, and stating that you have reached your final position.

4. Applying pressure through a threat of the consequences which will follow if your offer is not accepted.
5. Giving your opponent a choice between two courses of action.

Do not make a final offer unless you mean it. If it is not really your final offer and your opponent calls your bluff, you will have to make further concessions and your credibility will be undermined. He will, of course, attempt to force you into revealing how close you are to your final position. Do not allow him to hurry you. If you want to avoid committing yourself and thus devaluing the word 'final', state as positively as you can that this is as far as *you* are prepared to go.

Chapter 26

Objectives

Objectives are needed in every area where performance and results directly and vitally affect the survival and prosperity of a business (Peter Drucker).

In theory at least, the better you know where you are going, the more likely you are to get there. However, no organization has one simple objective such as to maximize profits. High profits in the short run would mean running down stocks and cutting back on investments which would endanger the company's future existence. A book club, for example, can only survive in the long run by 'investing' in new members. If it lived off the fat of existing members it could make more money in the short term but as these members left it would run out of income and go out of business. Survival and growth are thus prime objectives, along with that of maximizing profit.

The problem facing most organizations — profit or non-profit making — and their managers is one of balancing the various objectives and deciding on priorities.

A company may express its objectives under a number of headings, for instance:

☐ To increase market share to x per cent
☐ To maintain return on capital employed at its present level
☐ To increase turnover in real terms by x per cent
☐ To maintain profit as a percentage of sales at its present level
☐ To launch product A by a given date, achieving a return on investment of £x in the first year.

Stating objectives in this way is only a starting point. Policies and plans on how to achieve objectives and reconcile conflicts between them will have to be evolved. And this will mean evaluating alternatives and, sometimes, keeping options open when the information is not available on which an immediate decision can be made.

Why have objectives?

As Peter Drucker points out, objectives in a business enterprise enable management to explain, predict and control activities in a way which single ideas like profit maximization do not. More specifically, objectives:

- ☐ Enable the organization to explain the whole range of business phenomena in a small number of general statements
- ☐ Allow the testing of those statements in actual performance
- ☐ Enable decisions to be examined while they are still being made rather than after they have been effected
- ☐ Help to improve future performance by the analysis of past experience.

Corporate objectives

Peter Drucker has suggested that there are eight areas in which performance objectives should be set: market standing, innovation, productivity, physical and financial resources, profitability, manager performance and development, worker performance and attitude, and public responsibility. One other key area is overall activity levels as measured by sales. Any board would be well advised to sit down at least once a year and use these headings as an agenda for considering the future. Then they should review achievements against objectives at regular intervals during the year.

Some objectives such as market share, profits as a percentage of turnover, sales turnover, and sales turnover per employee are quantifiable as targets. Others, such as launching a new product, can be set as aims to be achieved by a certain date. In areas such as manager and worker performance where a target cannot be quantified or defined, it is still useful to have a broad statement of aims.

Individual objectives

There is no doubt that as a manager you will be in a better position to plan your work and monitor progress if you have clear objectives which have been agreed with your boss. It is equally certain that your subordinates will be more effective if they also understand and accept their objectives.

The table shows some of the headings under which objectives can be formulated in different jobs.

General Manager	Works Manager	Sales Manager
Profitability	Achievement of factory output targets	Achievement of sales targets
Volume and growth of business	Control of costs	Contribution to profits and fixed overheads
Provision and utilization of fixed assets	Utilization of plant and machinery	Development of new accounts
Provision and utilization of current assets	Control of stocks	Extension of existing business
Product innovation	Product quality	Customer satisfaction
Customer satisfaction	Labour productivity	Identification of new products
Operating costs	Industrial relations	Introduction of new products
Management effectiveness	Management effectiveness	Effectiveness of sales force
Employee productivity and attitude	Safety	Control of costs

When setting your own or other people's objectives you should avoid quantification for quantification's sake. Artificial figures attached to objectives are unhelpful. To ask a personnel manager to reduce the rate of absenteeism from 4.3 per cent to 4.0 per cent is to give him a meaningless objective. He cannot predict with precision how any action he takes will affect absence levels. It would be far better to set a broad objective such as 'to work with line management and the company's medical officer to develop procedures which will reduce the level of absenteeism'. His success can then be measured by the extent to which absenteeism has been reduced, not by his ability to achieve an arbitrary figure.

The other thing to avoid in setting individual objectives is to create too much paperwork. Discuss and agree objectives with your subordinates; review results against those objectives; agree what has to be done to improve performance and what changes need to be made to current objectives. But don't use elaborate forms for the purpose. All you need to record can be put down on one side of one sheet of paper — in handwriting.

159

Above all, remember that what you are trying to do is to provide a guideline for future action. Objectives are only worth setting for yourself or other people if they are used as the basis for plans and for monitoring performance.

Chapter 27
Organizing

The task

Your job as a manager is to develop an organization which gets the work done as you want it to get done. Organizing is basically about who does what. It means defining responsibilities, building structures and developing relationships. The essential element is people: what they do and how they work together.

Organizations are not static things. Changes are continually taking place in the business itself, in the environment in which the business operates and in the people who work in the business. This makes it difficult, if not impossible, to achieve an ideal organization. It is a good thing to have an ideal structure in mind, but you will have to modify it. How you modify it depends on the circumstances, and, especially, on people. For example, you will probably be forced to accept the fact that at senior levels you are going to have to build your organization around the capacities, strengths and even weaknesses of the people you've got — in the short term at least.

Basic approaches to organization design

When you are setting up a new organization structure or considering the effectiveness of an existing one, it is advisable to:

1. Define what the organization is there to do
2. Analyse the circumstances in which the activities are carried out — the technology, the rate of growth or change, the sort of management and its management style, and the outside environment
3. Identify the activities required to achieve the aims of the organization
4. Group related activities logically together into

organizational units and, within these units, into individual positions
5. Establish the relationships that should exist in the organization — vertically within functions and horizontally between functions — paying particular attention to the need to integrate the work of related activities
6. Ensure that everyone in the organization understands what they have to do (responsibilities), how far they can go in doing it (authority), the structure in which they operate, and the relationships they are expected to maintain.

The process of structuring a new organization or re-structuring an existing one is akin to building something with a box of bricks. The bricks are the key activities or groups of closely related activities. So the first thing to do is to define what these bricks are. In other words, you carry out an activity analysis. You then need to fit them together to build your structure. And there will be several ways in which the bricks — ie the discrete activities — can be grouped together. You may have to experiment with alternative arrangements to decide which pattern looks the best. It may well be a matter of choosing between two or three structures which look equally good, and the decisive factor is likely to be the quality of the people you have got or can obtain.

Organization guidelines

The following guidelines are intended to help you deal with organizational problems.

Formal and informal organizations
A formal organization can be described as a system of coordinated activities in which groups of people work cooperatively under authority and leadership towards a common goal. Formal structures aim to achieve orderly relationships between functions, but they also have the added value of providing people with a sense of security. The boundaries between functions should never be allowed to become barriers to communication.

An informal organization always exists alongside the formal one. People behave and interact in ways which cannot be defined in manuals, charts and job descriptions. They cross lines and cut corners. They set up informal groups which extend over organizational boundaries. This fluidity within the organization is a valuable characteristic. It nearly always helps the organization to achieve its aims. If, on occasion, it creates confusion and conflict, then something has to be done to resolve these problems without jeopardizing people's freedom to organize themselves informally.

Structure and function

The appropriate type of organizational structure is determined by the nature of the work carried out, and the conditions in which the company operates. The structure should be designed to facilitate the identification and accomplishment of work and to enhance the ability of employees to work together.

Formal, well defined and highly structured or bureaucratic organizations may well be appropriate where conditions are stable and predictable. Changeable situations may demand organizations which are more fluid, less rigidly defined and organic in the sense that their form develops in line with changes in their functions.

Different structures can exist in the same organization: a bureaucratic (formal) structure may be appropriate for some tasks and a non-bureaucratic (informal) structure for others.

Allocation of work

The work that needs to be done has to be defined and allocated to the appropriate job holders or departments. Related activities should be grouped together to avoid unnecessary overlap and duplication of work.

Matters requiring a decision should be dealt with as near to the point of action as possible.

Managers should not try to do too much themselves. Neither should they exercise too close supervision.

Levels in the structure

Too many levels of management and supervision inhibit communication and create unnecessary work (and jobs). Your aim should be to reduce the number of levels to a minimum, bearing in mind always that organizations are like india rubber — if you squeeze them they will expand sideways, ie at some levels the number of subordinates directly reporting to one manager will increase.

Span of control

There are limits to the number of people anyone can manage or

163

supervise well. These vary considerably between different jobs. Most people can work with a far greater span of control than they think they can, as long as they are prepared to delegate more effectively and avoid getting into too much detail.

One man — one boss
Generally speaking, individuals should report to only one boss. This avoids conflicting orders being given to one person. If a manager bypasses his immediate subordinate when issuing instructions, it can cause confusion, and it undermines authority. If it happens too often, you will need to question the abilities of the manager and his subordinate, and the existence of the intermediate layer of management. Of course, there may be occasions when bypassing has to take place to deal with an emergency, but these should be exceptional.

The exception to the 'one man — one boss' principle is the case of 'functional authority'. For instance the finance director may lay down methods of preparing budgets and pass instructions on budgeting direct to managers in other departments. But functional authority should only be exercised as a means of getting company-wide policies which have been agreed at top level implemented consistently.

As long as the nature of the authority is understood by all concerned, there should be no confusion. If, however, anyone feels that he has received an unreasonable request from a functional manager, he is at liberty to appeal to his own line manager.

Organization charts

Charts are sometimes useful in planning and reviewing large organizations. They indicate how work is allocated and how activities are grouped together they show who is responsible to whom and they illustrate lines of authority. Drawing up a chart can be a good way of clarifying what is currently happening: the mere process of putting the organization down on paper will highlight any problems. And when you come to considering changes, charts are the best way of illustrating alternatives.

The danger with organization charts is that they can be mistaken for the organization itself. They are a snapshot of what is supposed to be happening at a given moment. They are out of date as soon as they are drawn and they leave out the informal organization. If you use little boxes to represent people, they may behave as if they were indeed little boxes, sticking too closely to the book of rules.

Charts can make people very conscious of their superiority or inferiority to others. They can make it harder to change things, they can freeze relationships, and they can show relationships as they are supposed to be, not as they are. Townsend said of organization charts: 'Never formalize, print and circulate them. Good organizations are living bodies that grow new muscles to meet challenges.'

Use organization charts carefully if at all. They can do more harm than good.

Job descriptions

Like organization charts, job descriptions can be too rigid and stifle initiative. If kept brief (one side of one sheet of paper) they have their uses: to define the sort of job for which you are recruiting — and the sort of person you want to find; to provide a basis for training programmes and performance appraisal and to help slot jobs into a pay structure.

But the elaborate, three-, four- and five-page efforts that are produced in some companies are a waste of time, especially at senior levels. Townsend again: 'Judgement jobs are constantly changing in nature and the good people should be allowed to use their jobs to see how good they are.' If, say, a production manager needs a four-page job description to tell him how to make widgets, he should not be a production manager.

The danger of written job descriptions is that people feel restricted by them. They might feel that they ought not to do unspecified work because they have no responsibility or authority beyond their written list of duties. Of course, any able executive who tries to can bend a job description to suit his own purposes. And the problem can be avoided altogether by inserting a catch-all phrase into the job description to the effect that the job holder will 'carry out such other duties as are required to achieve the overall purpose of the job'.

Job descriptions are frequently consigned to the files and forgotten about as soon as they are written. If and when they are resurrected, they are out of date. This is the most powerful argument against lengthy job descriptions — they are a waste of time and money.

Job descriptions should be brief, handwritten, used for a specific purpose such as those mentioned above, and then scrapped.

Case studies

The type of organization structure you need will depend on the type of operation you are in. The following two cases were mentioned by Honor Croome in *The Human Problems of Innovation*. They were based on research carried out in Scotland by Tom Burns and G. M. Stalker.

The first case illustrates organization problems as perceived by a manager in a firm which was mainly engaged in high technology development and batch production work. The second is a description of how organization in a process plant operated smoothly.

The case of the harassed high technology manager

Here, in interview, is an executive concerned with the design, production and sale of an advanced product; his department produces, designs, controls progress through the works, buys in stock and parts, and runs a separate assembly plant, using components produced elsewhere in the works. He has been having trouble in sales and production and he ascribes these troubles precisely to the lack of a clear-cut, up-and-down, structure of responsibility.

'Well, to my mind, the most important thing is delegation of authority and responsibility to the different levels from whoever is resident at the top. In our case it would be the managing director. Now the authority must be in line with the responsibility that you expect the individual to take . . . . One man holding all the strings and under him a sound team of people who are specialists in the various fields and in the various management functions which they are to exercise . . . .

'What happens in our case, the way I see it, is that this top management layer is missing and you're jumping virtually from managing director to a number of senior technicians in charge of section . . . who haven't got anyone coordinating their efforts except the managing director by his occasional appearances and periodic meetings . . . . Now to take one instance, we do have meetings. They are fashionable now. Something goes wrong and then it's decided that a weekly meeting should take place.'

'What kind of things go wrong?'

'Well, supposing that a delivery goes wrong, or a design is put into production and is functionally not quite what it ought to be, then there is the usual post-mortem and it usually boils down to that everybody realizes there hasn't been enough control. People have gone too far and got rather wrapped up in their own particular small aspect of the overall project. It's then realized that there hasn't been any one body keeping an overall eye on things, and the usual scheme is to inaugurate a weekly meeting at which various points can be raised and discussed. Now, in theory, that's a very desirable thing so long as it discusses matters relative to its function. Also that the plan of attack for the following week's work is clearly laid down and it is stated who will do what and they report back. It shouldn't just amount to a weekly gathering of bodies who, half-way through the meeting, drink a cup of tea and then break up and that's that . . . .'

'What kind of things go wrong that are not put right at such meetings?'

'Well, when you start a new design there are certain steps you must go through to get a new production batch on the go. Those steps involve the drawing office, purchasing, and planning and progress. That in turn will require examination of the capacity within the plant, machine loading and the rest . . . . To get the whole thing going needs one instruction to one man who, in turn, will see that the wheels are set in motion. Well, that doesn't normally happen here. There is no one man. What it amounts to is that it's announced "Wouldn't it be a good idea if we produced another ten of such and such a type?" and everybody says, "Yes, Sir, it's a jolly good idea. Let's do that." The meeting breaks up, and a few days later, for instance, I'm in the drawing office and happen to say, "What have you done about those ten units?" and they'll say, "Haven't had any instructions." I say, "Well, you go ahead and get the drawings printed and the schedules out." The chap in charge of the drawing office will take my word for it — *not* because he has been instructed that I will give him his instructions but because I've always done so off my own bat and I know that unless somebody tells him he'll stay put.

'That may be the first movement. The lot will go forward to purchasing. Stock control first will run through the schedules, tick off what is in stock and so forth — there is an automatic passage of the schedule through the various departments. Ultimately somebody, usually it's the stores, will say, "Well, there's a hell of a lot of stuff in for the job. When are you going to start it?" Then everybody will think, "When are we going to start it?" Because, at the time when I said to Charlie in the drawing office, "It's time you got your schedules out, boy", nobody said to the planning office, "How are we going to fit this job in?" People here are not pushing their jobs through but trying to drag them out the other end, like a surgeon with a pair of forceps trying to drag the baby out . . . .

'And our own production manager has no direct control over machining facilities. Whatever he gets done in other shops he has to try to ease in or bolster his way round to try to get them in because there is nothing laid down. I mean, he would go and see the works manager and the planning people but the situation changes so fast, he wouldn't be in the picture all the time. They wouldn't keep him informed; they'd say, "All right, we can put so and so in the machine shop on — you can have them." And twenty minutes later maybe something else comes up, they take his job off and put the new thing on, and nobody would tell him. So two days later he'd come back and ask how the job was getting on. They might be sorry, they might not, but it wasn't their affair really . . . .'

The harassed executive saw his firm's troubles as stemming from the lack of a proper line of command. But what his account shows is that his firm had to deal with tasks which could not be handled in this way. The 'functional contact' whose absence he deplored could not possibly, given the sort of work that the firm was doing, be satisfactory if it was a merely or even mainly up-and-down or 'vertical' kind, a matter of clear-cut authority and limited powers.

Yet no other way was thought feasible. When the command system showed signs of strain, a progress committee had been formed as a first move towards another kind of system which would allow of a bigger, less specified contribution from the executives concerned. Even during the meetings, however, the management group had reverted to the command system. They had looked to the managing director for decisions — 'Yes, Sir, that's a jolly good idea' — and for the allocation of a specific job to each of them.

The case of the process production firm
This firm produced rayon filament yarn, using processes which had once been scientifically advanced, but were not thoroughly assimilated into routine production.

Production started with the intake of raw materials (cellulose, carbon bisulphide, sulphuric acid, etc) and the first stage was the arrangement of the stored cellulose sheets into batches of uniform weight. From the weighing machine the cellulose was hand-carted to a vat of caustic solution in which it was steeped for a certain time; after steeping, it was pressed between plates by a hydraulic ram, then carted and fed into the mechanical kneaders. The shredded cellulose was then stored for two or three days in mercerizing rooms, to ensure a homogeneous moisture content, before the next process, where it was mixed with carbon bisulphide in mechanical churns. The resulting product, cellulose xanthate, was dropped through chutes into mixers, in which it was dissolved in a solution of caustic soda and mixed into a homogeneous fluid — viscose. This viscose was then stored under vacuum to remove bubbles; then filtered; and stored again in charge tanks.

This completed the preparatory phase. The next, central, stage consisted in pumping the viscose through a multiple jet into a bath of sulphuric acid, from which it emerged as solid fibres. These were drawn up over a wheel, twisted into thread, and passed down into a spinning pot in which the thread was built up into cylindrical cakes. The cakes were then washed with neutralizing solutions and water, dried in heated lockers, inspected, weighed and despatched.

This sequence was a matter of mechanical and muscular efforts and of chemical action, each transforming or 'translating' the raw material a stage further. Alongside it, there took place a set of other actions, mostly a matter of human judgement though some were automatic, designed to keep the sequence running properly and smoothly. The spinning machine was automatic, but was tended by workers who stopped and started it in order to renew broken threads, remove completed cakes and replace empty pots. Thermostatic apparatus controlled heat and humidity in the mercerizing rooms and kept a record; workers were employed to inspect these and other records and report fluctuations outside a certain latitude. Samples were taken every hour from the baths of sulphuric acid; these were analysed in the laboratory, and any fluctuations beyond certain limits were noted and resulted in instructions to the foreman in charge to vary appropriately the input of sulphuric acid. At all stages these controls aimed at keeping the processing changes, and the conditions affecting these changes, within a range of permitted tolerances and as close as possible to a set of ideal constants.

These constants and tolerances were set down in a book (known as the 'Factory Bible') which was in the hands of every department head. It enshrined the norm to which it was everyone's duty to make that part of the process for which he was responsible conform. The process of correcting deviations might be extremely simple; the simplest corrections of all were automatic (thermostatic control). Almost as simple were the actions of a single worker replacing a clogged jet. The laboratory tests were rather more complex, and certain adjustments designed to reconcile technical variations with the production programme involved an elaborate system whose operation took up most of the works manager's time. At the top, the general manager in turn reconciled variations in the operation of production — by means of his control over the various sections within the works — with the requirements of the sales and costing departments and the board of directors.

The whole concern, in fact, can be seen as a three-sided pyramid of power, technical expertise, and knowledge of circumstances. At every step down from the top there was less authority, less technical expertise and less information. Each person's task was clearly laid down and defined by his superior. He knew just what he could do in normal circumstances without consulting anyone else; just what point of deviation from the normal he should regard as the limit of his competence; and just what he should do when this limit was reached — ie report to his superior. The whole system was devised to preserve normality and stability. The downward flow of instructions and orders, and the upward flow of reports and requests for such instructions and orders, were precisely and clearly channelled; it has the characteristics of a smoothly working automatic machine. Since everyone knew both his job and its limits, there was little consultation; contacts ran up and down, from subordinates to superior and vice versa, and the great majority of those contacts resulted in the giving of definite orders. The outstanding characteristics of the structure were that it was mechanical and authoritarian. And it worked very well.

Chapter 28
Persuading

A manager's job is 60 per cent getting it right and 40 per cent putting it across. Managers spend a lot of time persuading other people to accept their ideas and suggestions.

Persuasion is just another word for selling. You may feel that good ideas should sell themselves, but life is not like that. Everyone resists change and anything new is certain to be treated with suspicion. So it's worth learning a few simple rules that will help you to sell your ideas more effectively.

Six rules for effective persuasion

1. *Define your objective and get the facts*: Decide what you want to achieve and why. Assemble all the facts you need to support your case. Eliminate emotional arguments so that you and others can judge the proposition on the facts alone.

2. *Find out what 'he' wants*: Never underestimate a person's natural resistance to change. But bear in mind that such resistance is proportional, not to the total extent of the change, but to the extent to which it affects him personally. When asked to accept a proposition, the first questions people ask themselves are: 'How does this affect me?' 'What do I stand to lose?' 'What do I stand to gain?' These questions must be answered before persuasion can start.

   The key to all persuasion and selling is to see your proposition from the other man's point of view. If you can really put yourself into the other man's shoes you will be able to foresee objections and present your ideas in the way most attractive to him.

   You must find out how he looks at things — what he wants. Listen to what he has to say. Don't talk too much.

Ask questions. If he asks you a question reply with another question. Find out what he is after.

Then present your case in a way that highlights its benefits to him, or at least reduces his objections or fears.

3. *Prepare a simple and attractive presentation*: Your presentation should be as simple and straightforward as possible. Emphasize the benefits. Don't bury the selling points. Lead him in gently so there are no surprises. Anticipate objections.

4. *Make him a party to your ideas*: Get him to contribute, if at all possible. Find some common ground in order to start off with agreement. Don't antagonize him. Avoid defeating him in argument. Help him to preserve his self-esteem. Always leave him a way out.

5. *Positively sell the benefits*: Show conviction. You are not going to sell anything if you don't believe in it and communicate that belief. To persuade effectively you have to sell yourself. You must spell out the benefits. *What* you are proposing is of less interest to the individual concerned than the effects of that proposal on him.

6. *Clinch and take action*: Choose the right moment to clinch the proposal and get out. Make sure that you are not pushing too hard, but when you reach your objective don't stay and risk losing it. Take prompt follow-up action. There is no point in going to all the trouble of getting agreement if you let things slide afterwards.

Chapter 29
Planning

Its uses and limitations

Planning is an attempt to shape the future. You decide where you want to arrive and how you will provide the resources you will need to get there. But because it deals with the future it has its limitations. Winston Churchill summed them up when he said: 'It is wise to plan ahead but difficult to look further than you can see.'

In a splendidly iconoclastic chapter of his book *The Naked Manager* Robert Heller had a go at the cult of long-range planning. 'What goes wrong', he wrote, 'is that the sensible anticipation gets converted into foolish numbers: and their validity always hinges on large loose assumptions.'

Plenty of examples can be quoted of planners getting it wrong. The oil industry regularly fails to forecast changes in oil prices. The British fertilizer company, Fisons, plunged into ambitious corporate planning and ended up with huge over-capacity and tiny profits. The educational planners in Great Britain made grossly wrong assumptions about the future birth rate and ended up with too many well and expensively trained teachers chasing too few jobs.

The future is always obscure but that does not obviate the need to plan. It just means that you must be cautious about committing yourself too heavily to any course of action which relies on unreliable assumptions about the future.

The main advantages of long-range corporate planning, even when it is based on fallible assumptions, is that it gives you a sense of direction, a purpose in life and an idea of the resources you will need in the future. Unrealistic planning can be avoided if you limit your planning to a period over which you can forecast trends with reasonable accuracy and regularly update your plans when conditions change.

173

At managerial level the virtues of planning ahead are self-evident. Your problem is to ensure that your plans are realistic and are integrated with the corporate plans. Corporate and managerial planning are discussed below.

Corporate planning

In corporate or long-range planning the time scale will vary from twenty years for the oil industry, five years or more for processing or mass production companies, up to three years for batch production firms and only one year or so for trading concerns which are at the mercy of the market and do not need much capital investment. The time scale of the plan will depend on the accuracy with which the future can be forecast and the time needed to launch new products or services, to enter new markets or to obtain new capital equipment or property.

Long-range plans are simply financial forecasts giving projections of turnover, expenses, profit, capital investment and the balance sheet. It is when these financial projections are accompanied by detail on how the results will be achieved that they become corporate plans. These will include programmes for the introduction or deletion of products, plans for entering new markets and plans for getting the resources required — finance, people, space, plant and equipment.

Corporate planning consists of the following six stages:

Stage 1. Define the business you are in

You may think you are in publishing, but you could really be in the leisure or educational business. An analysis of the business you are in helps you to understand the existing and potential market and to redefine methods of appraising it. If a paperback publisher says that he is in the leisure business he is recognizing that he is competing for the disposable income of consumers. His plans should lead towards an increasing share of the leisure market. The analysis should identify what you are good at so that you can concentrate on exploiting excellence.

Stage 2. Define corporate objectives

In a profit making company the overall objective may be to maximize the return to the shareholders in the form of capital growth. But this primary aim needs to be expanded.

You could usefully follow the example of Owen Green the chairman of BTR, a conglomerate which over a decade increased sales from £50 million to £510 million and net profit from £1.5 million to £43 million. His 'ethic' is:

☐ Growth is the objective
☐ Profit is the measure
☐ Security is the result.

But you need to be more precise than that. Corporate economic objectives in a trading company could be to:

☐ Increase the return on capital employed from 15 per cent to 20 per cent by 19 . .
☐ Achieve a minimum annual increase in turnover of 10 per cent in real terms.

In an insurance company a broad statement of objectives might read:

'To achieve and maintain an optimum return on increasing capital employed the return must be such as:
a) to give shareholders an increasing return on their investments which compares favourably with the return available by investing elsewhere;
b) to be consistent with the company's obligations to its policy holders.'

Stage 3. External appraisal
External appraisal means analysing the environment in which the company operates — the economy, competition, government policies and market trends. The aim is to identify the key factors for success in present markets and the opportunities for profitably entering new markets or introducing new products.

You should also be answering Drucker's two questions:

1. What are the restraints and limitations that make the business vulnerable, impede its full effectiveness and hold down its economic results?
2. What are we afraid of, what do we see as a threat to this business — and how can we use it as an opportunity?

An external appraisal should ensure that the company's plans are based on the clearest possible understanding of future market opportunities and possible threats from competition, government action or adverse economic trends.

In an insurance company this review would cover:

☐ Prospects for the economy, especially in interest rates

- ☐ The possible effects of government action on the business
- ☐ Trends in savings and cover against risk generally
- ☐ Population growth and changes in consumer taste
- ☐ An appraisal of competitors, especially banks and building societies.

Stage 4. Internal appraisal

The fourth stage of strategic planning is a step-by-step analysis of the company's strengths and weaknesses. Each activity should be taken in turn — sales, products, level of service, development and so on — and the following questions answered:

- ☐ *Strengths*
  - — What are the company's strengths (expertise and achievement)?
  - — How else could they be exploited?
  - — What would be the effect on profitability of further exploiting the strengths?
- ☐ *Weaknesses*
  - — What are the company's weaknesses?
  - — How can they be overcome?
  - — What would be the effect on profitability of overcoming them?

Stage 5. Alternative courses of action

The next stage is to identify possible strategies. The important thing at this stage is to let every possible idea come to the surface. The more practical ideas can then be selected and objectives set for them. The resources and time scale required to implement them can also be defined.

When assessing alternatives you need to take three factors into account: uncertainty, risk, and availability of resources.

Uncertainty is in the nature of things. Dr Johnson said: 'He is no wise man who will quit a certainty for an uncertainty.' Unfortunately, in business you have to do this all the time. Long-range plans can only give you a general outline of the way ahead and enable you to be prepared for eventualities. Uncertainty remains, and to deal with it contingency plans are often necessary. You must also ensure that plans are flexible and updated regularly or whenever conditions change.

Risk arises from uncertainty, but risks need to be classified. Drucker suggested that there are essentially four kinds of risk:

- ☐ The risk one must accept, the risk that is built into the

business
- [ ] The risk one can afford to take
- [ ] The risk one cannot afford to take
- [ ] The risk one cannot afford not to take.

He goes on to say: 'To lose money and effort spent in pursuit of an opportunity should always be a *risk one can afford to take.* If the money required is more than a company can lose and survive, it cannot afford the opportunity.'

Uncertainty and risk are what makes planning an art rather than a science. Your assessment of them will determine how you allocate resources to any new development or project. The availability of resources will be a limiting factor. Planning is very much concerned with the optimum use of those resources as well as with determining a course of events.

Stage 6. Convert the plan to action

The final stage is to prepare action programmes which will achieve agreed objectives and deadlines without exceeding the limits placed on the use of resources. Priorities and target dates should be set and responsibilities for managing and coordinating the programme allocated. Each manager should know what action is required of him and when. He should also know what resources he can use and how he should report back on progress.

Summarizing the plan

The plan should be summarized under four main headings:

1. *Business development* — to cover expansion and withdrawals in markets and products, diversifications and technical development
2. *Organization* — to decide what activities have to be carried out and outline a structure which will cater for them
3. *Resources* — the finance, manpower and facilities required
4. *Operations* — the detailed operating targets and budgets for each activity and department.

When planning goes wrong

Planning goes wrong either because people are over-confident about their ability to predict and shape the future, or are over-ambitious. Robert Heller in *The Business of Success* has six prescriptions for a company suffering from either of these diseases.

- [ ] Stick to a basic theme
- [ ] Concentrate short-term activity on improving basic efficiencies
- [ ] Couple short-term emphasis on efficiency with plans for medium- and long-term defence and improvement of market positions
- [ ] Use acquisition sparingly, either to strengthen the above tactics and strategies, or to add *immediately* to the return on assets
- [ ] Make stability, in management and in business development, a prime aim
- [ ] Last, but not least, never succumb to the notion that you're a genius: even if (which is unlikely) you are.

Managerial planning

As a manager you will normally plan ahead over a relatively short period of time – up to one or, at most, two years. And your objectives, targets and budgets will probably have been fixed by the corporate plan or company budget.

You plan to get things done on time without using more resources than you were allowed. Your aim should be to avoid crises and the high costs that they cause; to have fewer 'drop everything and rush this' problems. Planning warns you about possible crises and gives you a chance to avoid them. Contingency or fall-back plans should be prepared if you have any reason to believe that your initial plan may fail for reasons beyond your control.

When you plan, you choose certain courses of action and rule out others, that is to say you lose flexibility. This will be a disadvantage if the future turns out differently from what you expected – which is only too likely. Try to make plans that you can change at reasonable cost if you have to. It is a bad plan that admits no change.

Planning activities
As a manager, there are eight planning activities you need to carry out:

- [ ] *Forecasting*
    - What sort of work has to be done, how much and by when
    - How the work load might change

— The likelihood of the department being called on to undertake specialized or rush jobs

— Possible changes within or outside the department which might affect priorities, the activities carried out, or the work load

☐ *Programming* — deciding the sequence and time scale of operations and events required to produce results on time

☐ *Staffing* — deciding how many and what type of staff are needed and considering the feasibility of absorbing peak loads by means of overtime or temporary staff

☐ *Setting standards and targets* — for output, sales, times, quality, costs or for any other aspect of the work where performance should be planned, measured and controlled

☐ *Procedure planning* — deciding how the work should be done and planning the actual operations by defining the systems and procedures required

☐ *Materials planning* — deciding what materials, bought-in parts or subcontracted work are required and ensuring that it is made available in the right quantity at the right time

☐ *Facilities planning* — deciding on the plant, equipment, tools and space required

☐ *Budgeting.*

Planning techniques
Most of the planning you do as a manager is simply a matter of thinking systematically and using your common sense. Every plan contains three key ingredients:

☐ Objective — the innovation or improvement to be achieved
☐ Action programme — the specific steps required to achieve the right objective
☐ Financial impact — the effect of the action on sales, turnover, costs, and, ultimately, profit.

Here is an example of how a manufacturing plan could be set out:

Manufacturing Plan

Objective

To reduce the frequency and cost of faulty castings received from the XYZ Company.

Action Programme

Steps	Responsibility	Completion by
1. Ensure recognition by supplier of problem with 'hard spots' in castings.	Purchasing Manager Production Manager	15 January
2. Negotiate price concession on all castings received during weeks when we return more than ten bad castings.	Purchasing Manager	31 January
3. Set up storage area to accumulate ruined castings.	Facilities Manager	15 February
4. Establish procedures to record machine downtime and cutter breakage with individual castings.	Production Controller	1 March
5. Ensure XYZ Company agrees new arrangements.	Purchasing Manager	15 March

Profit Impact

		£ 19.. *Profit Increase (Decrease)*
Price concessions		7,000
Effect of improved quality	Scrap	8,500
	Overtime	3,500
	Expense tools	9,000
	Lost production	20,000
	Other	12,000
Modifications in storage area		(2,000)
Recording procedures		(1,000)
Other costs		(3,000)
	Total profit impact	£54,000

Bar charts should be used to express plans more graphically wherever there is more than one activity and care has to be taken to sequence them correctly. The manufacturing plan illustrated above could be expressed as follows:

Step (detailed in action programme	Responsibility	January	February	March
1. Get XYZ Company to recognize problem.	Purchasing Manager	▭		
2. Negotiate price concession.	Purchasing Manager		▭	
3. Set up storage area.	Facilities Manager		▭	
4. Establish downtime recording procedures.	Production Controller		▭	
5. Get XYZ Company to agree new arrangements.	Purchasing Manager			▭

A more refined method of planning activities in a complex programme, where many interdependent events have to take place, is network planning. This requires the recording of the component parts and their representation in a diagram as a network of interrelated activities. Events are represented by circles, activities by arrows and the time taken by activities by the length of the arrows. There can also be dotted arrows for dummy activities between events that have a time rather than activity relationship. A critical path can be derived which highlights those operations or activities which are essential for the completion of the project within the allocated time scale. An illustration of a basic network is given below.

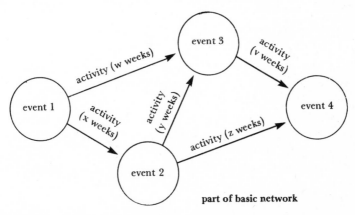

part of basic network

There may be occasions when even more sophisticated planning techniques using computer models, can be made available to help the manager, especially when large quantities of information have to be processed against a number of fixed

181

assumptions or parameters, or where alternative assumptions have to be assessed. In Book Club Associates, for example, the loading required in the warehouse in terms of machine time and man hours can be projected two years ahead by feeding parameters for projected activity levels into the programme. Plans can then be made to ensure that manpower and machine capacity is available to deal with forecast work levels.

Chapter 30
Policies

What are policies?

Anything which indicates what you can or cannot do in certain situations is a policy. It does not have to be written. It may not even have been stated explicitly. But if there is an understanding 'that this is the way we do things round here' then there is a policy.

For example, one business may lay down that 'company salary levels should be at the upper quartile of the range of salaries paid for comparable jobs elsewhere'. This is quite clear, although salary administrators can get bogged down in defining what is comparable and what is not.

Another business may have a salary structure which has developed in a more haphazard way. There may have been a general understanding that the company is prepared to pay above the going rate to get and to keep good quality staff, but nothing so precise as the upper quartile has been defined and nothing has been written down.

Both these companies have salary policies. Which of them has the best policy? There is only one answer to this question. The one that works. A clearly defined, almost rigid policy, quoting the upper quartile is fine if people find out what the upper quartile is and try their best to match it. Otherwise it is useless. A policy of paying above the going rate is great if that is what happens, and as long as the application of the policy is consistent between different jobs and different parts of the company.

Inconsistency is, of course, the danger of ill-defined policies. Just as undue restraint of judgement and initiative is the danger of a policy which is too rigid.

Why have policies?

When faced with a crisis or difficult decision it is helpful to have a guide. When running a business or a department it is essential to let people know what they can and cannot do.

A direct selling business will tell its agents in the field what they can do — they are to sell direct to housewives who are broadly in the middle income group. It will also tell them what they must not do — it is not the firm's policy to go in for high-pressure selling.

A retail store will tell its buyers what it wants them to do — to achieve a three times mark-up on the cost of the goods they purchase. It will also tell them what it does not want them to do — to sacrifice the firm's reputation for quality in the pursuit of low cost merchandise.

What makes a good policy?

A good policy is one that works. But what makes it work? In general, policies will work if they are appropriate — if they clearly take you in the direction you want to go. They need to be understood, which does not mean that they *have* to be written down. Oral tradition can be a more powerful force than an unused and dusty policy manual.

Policies need to be clear, which is easier said than done. If you try to be completely unambiguous you may only achieve a flood of words which defeat your purpose. Or, worse, your policy may become a prison rather than a pathway. There is a limit to how much you can or should spell out. Take this example:

> Divisional general managers may fix prices for the products under their control so long as:
> a) those prices produce gross profit margins in line with agreed budgets
> b) price reductions do not adversely affect prices in other divisions.

It looks clear enough, but is it? What does 'in line with' really mean? At what point are prices 'adversely affected'? There is scope for different interpretations in this definition. But is it clear enough? Yes. It gives the divisional managers concerned a general guideline sufficient to keep them from going off the rails. Some room for discretion is, however, allowed. And at this level, this is what policies must do. They should not act as strait-jackets.

Policies must have a degree of permanence or they are not really policies at all. If you constantly change them, no one, in or out of the organization, knows what to count on. But they should not become so hard and fast that they stop a company looking ahead. For example, a firm which holds to a policy of trading in the asbestos business is in danger if it ignores the fact that increased awareness of the risks of asbestos make it doubtful that there will be an asbestos business in a few years' time. A real example was British Airways' 'buy British' policy. They stuck to it rigidly until an inadequate choice of aircraft from British manufacturers and fierce competition forced them to buy abroad. But by then the profitability of the business had suffered considerably.

How to formulate policies

You cannot just sit down and say 'let's formulate a policy'. Policies should either emerge as a result of a series of decisions forced upon you by events or be part of a deliberate planning process which includes setting objectives and the broad strategies required to achieve them.

Policies should be formulated in response to needs: people require guidance on what or what not to do; plans can only be realized if the line to take is defined; points of reference are required in unfamiliar areas of decision making.

There is a lot to be said for defining policies in writing. But not in a vast policy manual which no one will read. Make your policy statement as clear and succinct as you can. Ensure that it gets to those who have to implement the policy and check that they understand the policy and are taking steps to put it into practice.

How to implement policies

If your policies are inappropriate or ambiguous the implementation will be hard. If not, all you need to do is to ensure that your staff are clearly briefed on what they are to do and how they are expected to do it. If there are areas left to their discretion, point this out. Less experienced staff may need more explicit guidance at this stage on how they should exercise their discretion. Give them an idea of the circumstances in which you would expect them to come to you for further guidance.

For example, a company introducing a 'promotion from within' policy might express it like this:

> Wherever possible, vacancies should be filled by the most effective people available from within the company subject to the right of the company to recruit from outside if there are no suitable internal candidates.

An experienced personnel officer would know what to do if, say, a departmental manager refused to release a member of his staff who had successfully applied for an internal vacancy. He would quote the policy without browbeating the manager with it, and use his powers of persuasion, based on past experience, to convince the manager to release the man. The inexperienced personnel officer, on the other hand, should be warned in advance that this problem might arise. He should be told not to rely too much on the rigid application of the policy. He should be instructed to use his discretion to decide whether he can gently persuade the manager, and if not, he must be prepared to go to the personnel manager for advice on how to handle the situation.

Once you have briefed staff all you need to do is to follow up and make sure that the policy is being applied properly and is appropriate. This gives you an opportunity for training your staff, or, if the policy is not working, for recommending amendments to it. You can only find out if a policy works by checking on how it works, and this means talking to the people who have to implement it.

Chapter 31
Power and politics

Power and politics in an organization go together. You may feel, like Nietzsche, that 'power has crooked legs'. But things don't get done without the exercise of authority, and authority requires the use of power. Furthermore, one way of getting authority and power is to indulge in company politics. You may deplore it, and many chief executives deny that it happens in their organizations. It does take place, however, because people seek power and often use political means to attain it.

Power – good or bad?

In his analysis of power in British industry, Anthony Jay commented: 'Power lies in the acceptance of your authority by others, their knowledge that if they try to resist you they will fail and you will succeed. Real power does not lie in documents etc – it lies in what you can achieve.'

And Mary Parker Follet wrote:'Our task is not to learn where to plan power; it is how to develop power. Genuine power can only be grown, it will slip from every arbitrary hand.'

Power is legitimate if it is used to pursue legitimate ends and is wielded in a responsible way by responsible people. But it can be employed in a harsh way, as in the following example quoted by John Kotter in the *Harvard Business Review.*

> When young Tim Babcock was put in charge of a division of a large manufacturing company and told to 'turn it around' he spent the first few weeks studying it from afar. He decided that the division was in disastrous shape and that he would need to take many large steps quickly to save it. To be able to do that, he realized he needed to develop considerable power fast over most of the division's management and staff. He did this in the following way.
>
> He gave the division's management two hours' notice of his arrival. He arrived in a limousine; his six assistants arrived by train. He immediately called a meeting of the 40 top managers. He

outlined his assessment of the situation, his commitment to turn things around, and the basic direction he wanted things to move in. Babcock then fired the four top managers in the room and told them that they had to be out of the building in two hours. He then said he would personally dedicate himself to sabotaging the career of anyone who tried to block his efforts to save the division. At the end of the 60-minute meeting he announced that his assistants would set up appointments for him with each manager, starting at 7.00 am the next day. Throughout the critical six-month period that followed, those who remained at the division generally cooperated energetically with Mr Babcock.

'Tough' does not necessarily mean 'bad'. In this case perhaps the end justified the means.

David McClelland's studies of power in action involving over 500 managers from 25 different US corporations led him to conclude:

> [Managers] must possess a high need for power, that is, a concern for influencing people. However, this need must be disciplined and controlled so that it is directed towards the benefit of the institution as a whole and not toward the manager's personal aggrandizement.... [Managers motivated by a need for power] are able to create a greater sense of responsibility in their divisions and, above all, a greater team spirit.

Here are two cases of power being used without the brutality of the example above:

> *Case 1:* One of the best managers we have in the company has lots of power based on one thing or another over most people. But he seldom if ever just tells or asks someone to do something. He almost always takes a few minutes to try to persuade them. The power he has over people generally induces them to listen carefully and certainly disposes them to be influenced. That, of course, makes the persuasion process go quickly and easily. And he never risks getting the other person upset by making what that person thinks is an unfair request or command.

> *Case 2:* Product manager Stein needed plant manager Billings to 'sign off' on a new product idea (Product X) which Billings thought was terrible. Stein decided there was no way he could logically persuade Billings because Billings just would not listen to him. With time, Stein felt, he could have broken through that barrier. But he did not have that time. Stein also realized that Billings would never, just because of some deal or favour, sign off on a product he did not believe in. Stein also felt it not worth the risk of trying to force Billings to sign off, so here is what he did:
>
> On Monday, Stein got Reynolds, a person Billings respected, to send Billings two market research studies that were very favourable to Product X, with a note attached saying, 'Have you seen this?

I found them rather surprising. I am not sure if I entirely believe them, but still . . . .'

On Tuesday, Stein got a representative of one of the company's biggest customers to mention casually to Billings on the phone that he had heard a rumour about Product X being introduced soon and was 'glad to see you guys are on your toes as usual'.

On Wednesday, Stein had two industrial engineers stand about three feet away from Billings as they were waiting for a meeting to begin and talk about the favourable test results on Product X.

On Thursday, Stein set up a meeting to talk about Product X with Billings and invited only people whom Billings liked or respected and who also felt favourably about Product X.

On Friday, Stein went to see Billings and asked him if he was willing to sign off on Product X. He was.

Sources of power

Power is clearly linked to position and rank. But to a certain degree it has to be earned. You can give orders to your subordinates but you are going to get more out of them if you obtain their willing cooperation rather than their grudging submission. Power is bestowed upon you as a manager but you have to justify your use of it.

There are, however, other sources of power, namely:

☐ *Access to other people with power*. Proximity or a direct line obviously gives you more scope to exert influence, actual or perceived. That is why secretaries are important.

☐ *Control over information*. 'Knowledge is power' or, alternatively, 'authority goes to the one who knows'. If you are in the know, you are in a better position to control events or, if you want to play politics, to put spokes in other people's wheels.

☐ *Control over resources*. If you have control over resources such as money, manpower, equipment or services that you or anyone else needs, you have power.

☐ *Control over rewards and punishments*. You also have power if you can give rewards or punishments or influence others who control them.

☐ *Expertise*. You gain and keep power if you can convince others that you are the expert.

☐ *Identification*. You can achieve power over others if you persuade them to identify with what you are doing or with you personally. This is what charismatic leaders do by enthusiasm, dedication, getting people involved and by sheer force of personality.

☐ *Sense of obligation*. If you develop a sense of obligation by doing favours for people you can reasonably expect that they will feel an obligation to return those favours.

Using power

John Kotter interviewed over 250 managers who were in a position to use power. He found that the successful ones had the following characteristics:

☐ They use their power openly and legitimately. They are seen as genuine experts in their field and consistently live up to the leadership image they build for themselves.
☐ They are sensitive to what types of power are most effective with different types of people. For example, experts respect expertise.
☐ They develop all their sources of power and do not rely too much on any particular technique.
☐ They seek jobs and tasks which will give them the opportunity to acquire and use power. They constantly seek ways to invest the power they already have to secure an even higher positive return.
☐ They use their power in a mature and self-controlled way. They seldom if ever use power impulsively or for their own aggrandizement.
☐ They get satisfaction from influencing others.

Politics – good or bad?

A politician is defined in the *Oxford English Dictionary* as 'a shrewd schemer; a crafty plotter or intriguer'. Company politicians can be like this. They manoeuvre away behind people's backs, blocking proposals they do not like. They advance their own reputation and career at the expense of other people's. They are envious and jealous, and act accordingly. They are bad news, and they should be stopped. Unfortunately, they work behind closed doors and can too easily scuttle away under the skirting board if you try to crush them. And so they continue to survive.

But politics of a much more gentle kind are also found in any organization. There are occasions when a subtle appeal rather than a direct attack will pay dividends; and sometimes you have to exercise your powers of persuasion indirectly on those whose support you need. The following case study illustrates the legitimate use of politics:

> James Hale was the personnel director of a large divisionalized group in the food industry. The rate of growth by expansion and acquisition had been very rapid. There was a shortage of really good managers and a lack of coordination between the divisions in the group and between those divisions and head office. Hale believed that setting up a group management training centre would be a good way of helping to overcome these problems. He knew, however, that he would have to get agreement to this plan not only from the managing director, who would be broadly sympathetic, but also from his co-directors. The MD would not act without the support of a majority on his board.
>
> In any case Hale genuinely felt that there was no point in developing a facility of this sort for people who were not interested in it. He therefore sat back and deliberately worked out a strategy for getting agreement to his proposal. He knew that a frontal attack might fail. Management development was perceived by his colleagues as a somewhat airy-fairy idea which had little relevance to their real concerns as directors. He therefore had to adopt a more subtle approach. He did not call it a political campaign, but that is what it was. He was setting out to influence people indirectly.
>
> The basis of his plan was an individual approach to each of his colleagues, adjusted to their particular interests and concerns. In the case of the marketing director, he got the general sales manager to advocate the need for training in sales management for divisional sales staff. He ran several pilot courses in hotels and invited the marketing director to the winding-up session. He made sure that the marketing director was impressed, not only by what the divisional sales staff had learned from the course, but also by the new spirit of identification with group aims and policies engendered by the training. Casually, the personnel director let slip the thought that if the group had its own training centre this feeling of commitment could be developed even more strongly.
>
> The same basic technique was used with the production director. In addition he was helped to come to the view that a centre owned by the group could speed up the introduction of new ideas and provide a facility for communicating directly with key staff which was not available at present.
>
> The finance director was a more difficult person to convince. He could easily assess the costs but found it difficult to accept largely subjective views of the potential benefits. In this case James Hale did not try too hard to persuade him against his will. He knew that the majority of the board was now in favour of the plan, including the managing director. Hale felt safe in leaving his financial colleague in an isolated and ultimately untenable position. The qualitative arguments, as absorbed by the other members of the board, including the managing director, had the ring of truth about them which no purely quantitative arguments could overcome.
>
> Hale was content that he had enough support. To clinch the

argument he played his last political card by warning the marketing and production directors that there might be some financial opposition. He then got them to agree with the thesis that they wouldn't allow 'Mr Money Bags' to adopt a narrow financial view and thus dictate the destiny of the firm.

James Hale had no difficulty in getting his proposal accepted at the next board meeting.

The non-legitimate use of politics

The following is an example of non-legitimate use of politics. Unfortunately, it is a fairly common one. In most organizations there are people who want to get on, and do not have too many scruples about how they do it. If it involves treading on other people's faces, then so be it.

Two directors of a company both aspired to be the next managing director. Mr Black, the finance director, had the ear of the MD. Mr White, the technical director, was more remote.

Mr White had a number of ideas for introducing new technology and had proved, to his own satisfaction at least, that the pay-off was considerable. Unfortunately he jumped the gun in order to anticipate comments from Black, and presented a paper to the managing director which was not as well argued as it might be. Black carefully lobbied the MD and convinced him that the proposal was full of holes — he also hinted that this was yet another example of White's inability to understand the wider commercial issues.

The MD accepted this view more or less completely and agreed with Black's suggestion that the whole proposal should be off-loaded on to a board sub-committee — a well known device to delay if not to stifle new ideas. This was done, and the introduction of new technology was unnecessarily delayed by 18 months. But Black had made his point as the practical man of affairs who would not allow the company to get involved in expensive and unrewarding projects.

Dealing with politics

The signs include:

☐ Back-biting
☐ Buck-passing
☐ Inexplicable delays in decision making which can only be attributable to background influences
☐ Hidden decisions
☐ The formation of cliques who gang up on people
☐ Feuding between people, and the division of the organization into armed camps
☐ Paper wars between armed camps — arguing by memoranda, a sign of distrust

☐ Snide comments or criticisms
☐ Excessive lobbying.

Having identified the behaviour, find out who the politicians are, how they are working and what they are trying to achieve. You may feel that a direct and open confrontation might clear the air and put an end to the intrigue.

On the other hand, if the political forces ranged against you are powerful, a direct attack could misfire. In these circumstances you may be tempted to fight back with the same political weapons. This is a dangerous course for both you and the organization. Bring the argument out into the open whenever you can. Always try to avoid the trap of saying 'if I can't beat them, I'll join them'.

Chapter 32
Presentations and effective speaking

A manager's job usually includes giving formal or informal presentations at meetings, and addressing groups of people at conferences or training sessions. To be able to speak well in public is therefore a necessary management skill which you should acquire and develop.

The three keys to effective speaking are:

☐ Overcoming nervousness
☐ Thorough preparation
☐ Good delivery.

Overcoming nervousness

Some nervousness is a good thing. It makes you prepare, makes you think and makes the adrenalin flow, thus raising performance. But excessive nervousness ruins your effectiveness and must be controlled.

The common reasons for excessive nervousness are: fear of failure, fear of looking foolish, fear of breakdown, a sense of inferiority and dread of the isolation of the speaker. To overcome it there are three things to remember and six things to do.

Three things to remember about nervousness

☐ Everyone is nervous. It is natural and, for the reasons mentioned earlier, a good thing.
☐ Speaking standards are generally low. You can do better than the other fellow.
☐ You have something to contribute. Otherwise why should you have been asked to speak?

Six things to do about nervousness

- ☐ *Practise*. Take every opportunity you can get to speak in public. The more you do it, the more confident you will become. Solicit constructive criticism and act on it.
- ☐ *Know your subject*. Get the facts, examples and illustrations which you need to put it across.
- ☐ *Know your audience*. Who is going to be there? What are they expecting to hear? What will they want to get out of listening to you?
- ☐ *Know your objective*. Make sure that you know what you want to achieve. Visualize, if you can, each member of your audience going away having learned something new which he is going to put into practical use.
- ☐ *Prepare*.
- ☐ *Rehearse*.

Preparation

Allow yourself ample time for preparation in two ways. First, leave yourself plenty of low-pressure time; start thinking early — in your bath, on the way to work, mowing your lawn, any place where you can freely develop new ideas on the subject. Second, you should leave yourself lots of time actually to prepare the talk. There are eight stages of preparation.

1. Agreeing to talk
Do not agree to talk unless you know you have something to contribute to *this audience* on *this subject*.

2. Getting informed
Collect facts and arguments for your talk by: brainstorming and writing down all the points as they occur; reading up the subject; talking to colleagues and friends and keeping cuttings and files on subjects you may have to speak on.

3. Deciding what to say
Start by defining your objective. Is it to persuade, inform, interest or inspire? Then decide the main message you want to get across. Adopt the 'rule of three'. Few people can absorb more than three new ideas at a time. Simplify your presentation to ensure that the three main points you want to get across come over loud and clear. Finally, select the facts and arguments which best support your message.

Never try to do too much. The most fatal mistake any speaker can make is to tell everything he knows. Select and simplify using the rule of three.

4. Structuring your talk

Good structure is vital. It provides for continuity, makes your thoughts easy to follow, gives the talk perspective and balance and, above all, enables you to ram your message home.

The classic method of structuring a talk is to 'tell them what you are going to say — say it — tell them what you have said'. This is the rule of three in action again, as applied to attention span. Your audience will probably only listen to one third of what you say. If you say it three times in three different ways they will at least hear you once.

You were no doubt told at school that an essay should have a beginning, a middle and an end. Exactly the same principle applies to a talk.

Tackle the middle of your talk first and:

☐ Write the main messages on separate postcards
☐ List the points you want to make against each main message
☐ Illustrate the points with facts, evidence, examples and introduce local colour
☐ Arrange the cards in different sequences to help you decide on the best way to achieve impact and a logical flow of ideas.

Then turn to the opening of your talk. Your objectives should be to create attention, arouse interest and inspire confidence. Give your audience a trailer to what you are going to say. Underline the objective of your presentation — what *they* will get out of it.

Finally, think about how you are going to close your talk. First and last impressions are very important. End on a high note.

Think carefully about length, reinforcement and continuity. Never talk for more than forty minutes at a time. Twenty or thirty minutes is better. Very few speakers can keep people's attention for long. An audience is usually very interested to begin with (unless you make a mess of your opening) but interest declines steadily until people realize that you are approaching the end. Then they perk up. Hence the importance of your conclusion.

To keep their attention throughout, give interim summaries which reinforce what you are saying and, above all, hammer home your key points at intervals throughout your talk.

Continuity is equally important. You should build your argument progressively until you come to a positive and overwhelming conclusion. Provide signposts, interim summaries and bridging sections which lead your audience naturally from one point to the next.

5. Prepare your notes
The best sort of notes are the postcards used in preparing the talk. Each card should cover one section and include the main headings. Avoid using too many words on each, they will only confuse you.

Cards of this type can easily be referred to during your talk and should not distract your audience. It is quite a good idea, however, to write out your opening and closing remarks, in full, on separate cards. You can then learn these by heart, ensuring a confident start and a positive end to your presentation.

6. Prepare visual aids
As your audience will only absorb one third of what you say, if that, reinforce your message with visual aids. Appeal to more than one sense at a time. Flip charts, slides and so on all provide good back up, but don't overdo them and keep them simple. Too many visuals can be distracting, and too many words, or an over-elaborate presentation, will distract, bore and confuse your audience.

7. Rehearse
Rehearsal is vital. It instils confidence, helps you to get your timing right, enables you to polish your opening and closing remarks and to coordinate your talk and visual aids.

Rehearse the talk to yourself several times and note how long each section takes. Get used to expanding your notes without waffling. Never write down your talk in full and read it during rehearsal. This will guarantee a stilted and lifeless presentation.

Practise giving your talk out loud — standing up, if that is the way you are going to present it. Some people like to tape record themselves but that can be off-putting. It is better to get someone to hear you and provide constructive criticism. It may be hard to take but it could do you a world of good.

Finally, try to rehearse in the actual room in which you are going to speak, using your visual aids and with someone listening at the back to make sure you are audible.

8. Check and prepare arrangements on site
Check the visibility of your visual aids. Make sure that you know how to use them. Test and focus the overhead or slide projector. Brief your film projector operator and get him to run through the film to ensure that there are no snags.

If you are using slides in a carousel go through the lot to check that the sequence is right and none is upside down.

Be prepared for something to go wrong with your equipment. You may have to do without it at short notice. That is why you should not rely too much on visual aids.

Before you start your talk, check that your notes and visual aids are in the right order and to hand. There is nothing worse than a speaker who mixes up his speech and fumbles helplessly for his next slide.

Delivery

With thorough preparation you will not fail. You will not break down. But the way you deliver the talk will affect the impact you make. Good delivery depends on technique and manner.

Technique
Your *voice* should reach the people at the back. If you don't know that you can be heard, ask. Its distracting if someone shouts 'speak up'. Vary the pace, pitch and emphasis of your delivery. Pause before making a key point, to highlight it, and again afterwards to allow it to sink in. Try to be conversational. Avoid a stilted delivery. This is one reason why you should *never* read your talk. If you are your natural self the audience is more likely to be on your side. As Browning said: 'Best be yourself, imperial, plain and true.'

Light relief is a good thing if it comes naturally. People are easily bored if they feel they are being lectured, but you should never tell jokes unless you are good at telling jokes. Don't drag them in because you feel you must. Many effective and enjoyable speakers never use them.

Your *words* and *sentences* should be simple and short.

Your *eyes* are an important link with your audience. Look at them, measure their reaction and adjust to it. Don't fret if people look at their watches, it's when they start shaking them to see if they've stopped that you should start to worry.

Use *hands* for gesture and emphasis only. Avoid fidgeting. Don't put your hands in your pockets.

Stand naturally and upright. Do not stand casually. Be and look like someone in command. If you pace up and down like a caged tiger you will distract your audience. They will be waiting for you to trip over some equipment or fall off the edge of the platform.

Manner

Relax and show that you are relaxed. Convey an air of quiet confidence. Relaxation and confidence will come with thorough preparation and practice.

Don't preach or pontificate to your audience. They will resent it and turn against you.

Show sincerity and conviction. Obvious sincerity, belief in your message, positive conviction and enthusiasm in putting your message across count more than any technique.

Conclusions

- ☐ You can learn to become an effective speaker with practice. Seize every opportunity you get to develop your skills.
- ☐ Nervousness can be controlled by preparation and knowledge of technique.
- ☐ Good preparation is more than half the battle.
- ☐ Technique is there to help you to exploit your personality and style to the full, not to obliterate them.

Chapter 33

Problem solving and decision making

Problems and opportunities

It is often said that 'there are no problems, only opportunities'. This is not universally true, of course, but it does emphasize the point that a problem should lead to positive thinking about what is to be done now, rather than to recriminations. If a mistake has been made, the reasons for it should be analysed, to ensure that it does not happen again. But it is then water under the bridge.

Faced with a continuous flow of problems and decisions you may occasionally feel utterly confused. We all feel like that sometimes.

Improving your skills

How can you improve your ability to solve problems and make decisions? There are a few basic approaches you should use:

Improve your analytical ability

A complicated situation can often be resolved by separating the whole into its component parts. Such an analysis should relate to facts, although, as Peter Drucker points out, when trying to understand the root causes of a problem you may have to start with an opinion. Even if you ask people to search for the facts first, they will probably look for those facts that fit the conclusion they have already reached.

Opinions are a perfectly good starting point as long as they are brought out into the open at once and then tested against reality. Analyse each hypothesis and pick out the parts which need to be studied and tested.

Mary Parker Follett's 'law of the situation' — the logic of facts and events — should rule in the end. And although you may start out with a hypothesis, when testing it, use Rudyard Kipling's six honest serving men:

> I keep six honest serving men
> (They taught me all I knew)
> Their names are What and Why and When
> and How and Where and Who.

Adopt a systematic approach

Use the methods discussed in Chapter 6: analysing the situation, identifying possible courses of action, weighing them up and deciding what to do.

But do not expect the system to produce a black and white solution. Remember what Drucker says:

> A decision is a judgement. It is a choice between alternatives. It is rarely a choice between right and wrong. It is at best a choice between almost right and probably wrong — but much more often a choice between two courses of action neither of which is probably more nearly right than the other.

You should not expect, or even welcome, a bland consensus view. The best decisions emerge from a clash of conflicting points of view.This is Drucker's first law of decision making — 'one does not make a decision without disagreements'. You need a clash of opinion to prevent people falling into the trap of starting with the conclusion and then looking for the facts that support it.

Alfred P. Sloan of General Motors knew this. At a meeting of one of his top committees he said: 'Gentlemen, I take it we are all in complete agreement on the decision here.' Everyone round the table nodded assent. 'Then,' continued Mr Sloan, 'I propose we postpone further discussion of this matter until our next meeting to give ourselves time to develop disagreement and perhaps gain some understanding of what the decision is all about.'

Use your imagination

A strictly logical answer to the problem may not be the best one. Use lateral thinking, analogies and brainstorming, as described in Chapter 12, to get off your tramlines and dream up an entirely new approach.

Keep it simple

One of the first principles of logic is known as 'Occam's razor'. It states that 'entities are not to be multiplied without necessity'.

That is, always believe the simplest of several explanations.

Implementation
A problem has not been solved until the decision has been implemented. Think carefully not only about how a thing is to be done (by whom, with what resources and by when) but also about its impact on the people concerned and the extent to which they will cooperate. You will get less cooperation if you impose a solution. The best method is to arrange things so that everyone arrives jointly at a solution freely agreed to be the one best suited to the situation (the law of the situation again).

Problem solving and decision making techniques

Effective problem solving and decision making require the following steps:

1. *Define the situation.* Establish what has gone wrong or is about to go wrong.
2. *Specify objectives.* Define what you are setting out to achieve now or in the future as you deal with an actual or potential problem or a change in circumstances.
3. *Develop hypotheses.* If you have a problem, develop hypotheses about the cause.
4. *Get the facts.* In order to provide a basis for testing hypotheses and developing possible courses of action, find out what is happening now and/or what is likely to happen in the future. If different people are involved, get both sides of the story and, where possible, check with a third party. Obtain written evidence wherever relevant. Do not rely on hearsay.
    Define what is supposed to be happening in terms of policies, procedures or results and contrast this with what is actually happening. Try to understand the attitudes and motivation of those concerned. Remember that people will see what has happened or is happening, in terms of their own position. Obtain information about internal or external constraints that affect the situation.
5. *Analyse the facts.* Determine what is relevant and what is irrelevant. Establish the cause or causes of the problem. Do not be tempted to concentrate on symptoms rather than causes. Dig into what lies behind the problem. When analysing future events, try to make a realistic assessment

PROBLEM SOLVING AND DECISION MAKING

in terms of existing trends both within and outside the organization. But be careful not to indulge in crude extrapolations. Consider the various internal and external organizational and environmental factors which may affect future developments.

6. *Consider possible courses of action.* List the possible courses of action in the light of the factual analysis. Where appropriate, use brainstorming and creative thinking techniques to identify courses of action which may not be immediately evident.

7. *Evaluate possible courses of action.* Consider the possibilities, listing pros and cons and comparing anticipated results with your specified objectives. Evaluate the immediate and future consequences both inside and outside the organization. Compare costs with benefits. Assess how far the needs of those involved will be met and the extent to which your decisions will be acceptable. Consider the risk of creating dangerous precedents. Consider also the implications of any internal or external constraints that might exist. Ensure that all concerned participate in the evaluating and decision making process. Note, however, that the degree of participation will depend on the nature of the problem and the participation procedures and management style of the organization.

8. *Decide and implement.* Decide which, on balance, is the preferred course of action, and discuss it with those concerned. Consider carefully how the decision is likely to affect them. Decide on the method of presentation, giving the reasons for the decision and, so far as possible, allaying any fears. Before implementing the decision ensure that everyone who needs it gets the relevant information.

9. *Monitor implementation.* Check on how effectively the decision is being implemented. Obtain the reactions of those affected. Take corrective action where necessary.

203

Chapter 34
Productivity improvement

The benefits of improved productivity

Work measurement programmes usually show that staff not on an incentive scheme perform at about 50 to 60 per cent of the standard that can reasonably be expected from an average worker.

Barry Smith, of consultants A. Kearney, (*Management Today*, October 1977) found that 'productivity audits of manufacturing and distribution activities consistently pinpoint opportunities of improving output by from 25 to 40 per cent with much the same plant and human resources'. Similarly, clerical work measurement programmes can almost always save more than 15 per cent of staff without affecting output or quality. The scope for improvement is tremendous and so is the pay-off, as the following analysis shows.

Payroll as a percentage of sales	Percentage increase in profit before tax* from improvement in productivity of:			
	5%	10%	20%	40%
20	20	40	80	160
30	30	60	120	240
40	40	80	160	320
50	50	100	200	500

* Assumes a return on sales of 5 per cent.

The pay-off from improving productivity is high, but how can you achieve it?

The first thing to do is to overcome apathy. Both managers and work force must be persuaded somehow that they have a common interest in increasing output per head. This is a difficult exercise. It requires considerable powers of leadership from the top and this means positive programmes for motivating and involving all concerned to obtain their commitment to improvement.

A continuous drive for productivity is required and a productivity improvement programme based on a productivity audit should be the instrument.

Productivity improvement programme

The objective of a productivity improvement programme should be to achieve a significant change for the better in the relationship between outputs and inputs or, to put it another way, an improvement in the following ratio:

$$\frac{\text{performance achieved}}{\text{resources consumed}}$$

What are the factors for success?

A successful productivity improvement campaign depends on:

☐ A well-planned programme based on a productivity audit, with positive objectives and a clearly defined timetable
☐ A commitment on the part of management and supervisors to the programme
☐ The involvement of employees in the programme so that they are prepared, with suitable safeguards concerning their future, to participate in implementing it
☐ A recognition that the benefits resulting from the programme should be shared among everyone concerned: the organization, management and all other employees.

These are demanding criteria and they are not easily achieved. Things can go wrong. Managers, supervisors and other employees will all be suspicious of the programme. They will see it either as a device for exposing their inadequacies, an instrument for producing unacceptable change, or a threat to their livelihood. These are emotional reactions and, once emotion comes in at the door, reason goes out of the window. So communication, education, involvement and persuasion are essential aspects of the programme.

Even if your powers of persuasion are great and you manage to involve employees in the programme sufficiently to overcome their natural resistance to change, there are a number of mistakes to be avoided in implementing productivity improvements. These include:

- ☐ Making recommendations based on inaccurate information or conclusions
- ☐ Making recommendations on new equipment, methods or procedures without properly evaluating the cost-effectiveness of the proposals
- ☐ Making recommendations without properly evaluating the impact of changes on other departments
- ☐ Proposing changes without giving sufficient consideration to the reactions of those involved.

These are common, but avoidable, errors. Those responsible for productivity improvement programmes will be much less likely to commit them if they are made aware of the dangers in advance. This is why it is important to be quite clear about who runs the programme and how it should be conducted.

Who runs the programme?
The programme for improving productivity must be run by top management. They should set the objectives, define terms of reference, appoint the executive responsible for the programme, provide him with the resources he needs and monitor the results achieved.

A senior manager responsible directly to the chief executive should be in charge of the programme. Never use a committee. It will spend its time talking, not doing. The productivity executive will need help — from organization and methods, work study, personnel and accounts departments — and he should get his aides involved directly, rather than sitting them round a table to talk to one another. It may be necessary to set up small project teams comprising members of different departments to carry out tasks, but they should be given specific things to do.

The employment of outside consultants will have to be considered. You should normally only use them as an 'extra pair of hands' providing expertise and resources not necessarily available within the organization. But they should be kept under control. They are there to work under the direction of the productivity executive, not to pursue their own line.

Consultants are often used as hatchet men to put forward the unpleasant recommendations that no one else wants to make. This is a pity. If you believe in productivity, you should realize that its achievement may not always be a comfortable process. You ought to be prepared to take justified action yourself and not rely on others to do it for you.

When you have decided who runs the programme, make sure that they know what you want them to achieve and that they adopt a systematic approach along the lines of the following productivity audit checklist.

Productivity audit checklist

What to look for
When you conduct a productivity audit you should look first at performance:

1. Actual compared with company standards and trends
2. Actual compared with other organizations
3. Reasons for unsatisfactory performance, which should be listed under the following headings:

   — Poor planning, budgeting and control procedures
   — Inefficient methods or systems of work
   — Inadequate use of work measurement
   — Insufficient mechanization or inadequate plant and machinery
   — Poor management
   — Poorly motivated employees
   — Badly paid employees
   — Too many restrictive practices
   — Inadequate training
   — Excessive waste.

The audit should then examine the following areas. Each one should be checked to discover what *should* be done, to what extent it *is* being done; and comment on any remedial action required.

1. Planning, budgeting and control — check that:
   a) Productivity performance tasks and standards are clearly defined, attainable, accurate and measurable
   b) Individuals are fully aware of the targets and standards they are expected to achieve
   c) Manpower plans and budgets are specifically concerned with setting and achieving realistic productivity targets
   d) Control reports clearly identify variances and deviations from the plan
   e) Individuals are fully accountable for failures to achieve

targets or standards
f) Prompt corrective action is taken by management to deal with adverse variances or results.

2. *Work methods* — check that:
   a) A continuous programme of reviewing and improving work methods in all parts of the organization is in existence
   b) The method improvement programme has the support of management, trade unions and employees
   c) The programme is producing real improvements in productivity.

3. *Work measurement* — check that:
   a) Work measurement is used, wherever feasible, to develop standards, give better control information and improve methods and procedures
   b) Work measurement is used to provide the basis for effective incentive schemes.

4. *Technology* — check that:
   a) There is a constant search by management for ways of improving productivity by the use of new technology — mechanization, computerization and automation
   b) Investment in equipment or machinery is justified on a cost-benefit basis
   c) Use of existing equipment is managed to achieve maximum productivity.

5. *Management* — check that:
   a) Management is fully conscious of the need for productivity
   b) Management and supervisors take active and successful steps to improve the productivity consciousness of their staff
   c) Productivity performance is treated as a key criterion in assessing the capabilities and rewards of management and supervisors
   d) The organization of work ensures that decisions on key aspects of productivity are taken at the point where work is carried out and the impact is greatest
   e) Research into methods of improving productivity is an important function in the organization.

6. *Motivation and involvement* — check that:
   a) Employees are motivated by management and supervisors to achieve greater productivity

b) A continuous review is carried out by management into ways of improving motivation for productivity
c) Employees are involved in seeking ways of improving productivity
d) Employees appreciate that improvements in productivity benefit themselves as well as the company.

7. *Pay* — check that:
   a) Payment-by-results schemes are used wherever possible to boost productivity
   b) Payment-by-results schemes are kept under close review to ensure that they are cost effective
   c) Rewards to those not on payment-by-results schemes are related to achievement
   d) Schemes for sharing the rewards from increased productivity among employees are used to promote further gains in productivity.

8. *Restrictive practices* — check that:
   a) Productivity agreements are negotiated with trade unions to buy out restrictive practices
   b) The agreements are cost effective, that is that the value of improvements in productivity resulting from the elimination of restrictive practices outweighs the cost of buying them out.

9. *Training* — check that:
   a) Analyses of training needs concentrate on ways of improving productivity
   b) Training programmes are derived from such analyses
   c) All those who can benefit from training to improve their productivity, especially new employees, are given such training
   d) The impact of training is followed up to ensure that it is cost effective, that is that gains in productivity resulting from training outweigh the cost of training.

10. *Elimination of waste* — check that:
    a) There is a continuous attack led by top management on all forms of excessive manpower costs and wasteful use of manpower
    b) Work and method study is used to improve the use of manpower by introducing more efficient techniques, systems and procedures
    c) Increases of staff, enlargement of support departments and

the engagement of indirect workers is rigidly controlled
d) Managers and supervisors are held strictly accountable for
wasteful practices.

Implementing improvements

It will be much easier to implement improvements in productivity if the objectives of your programme are understood
and accepted by all concerned. Clear direction from the top and
a systematic approach to conducting investigations are also
important. But you will fail to achieve the results you want if
you cannot get your workforce involved in the programme.

If you can get your staff involved they will identify themselves with the results. This will reduce their natural resistance
to change and ensure their cooperation. It will become *their*
programme rather than something imposed upon them.

A case study

The following case study is taken from *How to Avoid the British
Disease* by Chatterton and Leonard. It concerns a Manchester-
based engineering firm whose order books are bulging despite a
recession in the industry.

> The works director, Mr Chatterton, encouraged by his managing
> director, Ken Buckley, has, over a period of ten years, tried to
> develop a cooperative relationship with the workforce. His aim was
> to eliminate the class differences which, as in so many industries,
> were seen to be hampering production.
>
> In the early 1970s management and the workforce were barely
> talking to each other; niggling disputes cropped up frequently with
> the inevitable result of low sales and a dismal return on capital.
> Morale was low, labour turnover high and the payment system had
> virtually broken down. Everyone was worse off.
>
> The chief executive and the board started to ask themselves
> simple questions. Is the form of organization to blame? What are the
> workforce reacting to, or against? Would a better approach make
> people work better? As a result of a careful appraisal, backed by a
> survey of shop-floor attitudes, a number of reforms were gradually
> introduced. At one level they read like clichés falling out of a
> management manual — job enrichment, incentives, involvement —
> but cumulatively they added up to something of a revolution.
>
> First, according to Mr Chatterton, the company has adopted a
> community style of management which concentrates on the natural
> groups that form in the working population, including the
> identification of natural group leaders. Second, the provision of
> information was increased. A fortnightly meeting is held with shop

stewards, even if there is nothing on the agenda, and stewards are encouraged to go on day-release courses to learn about the financial side of running a business.

If there is a problem, say of a technical nature, all of the people involved are brought together to talk it through with the objective of harnessing a wide spread of expertise to solve the problem, rather than trying to identify who was responsible.

Third, the company has tried to improve communications by flattening out the management structure from seven layers to five: managing director, works directors, works managers, foremen and the shop floor.

Staff have been given the freedom to go across the strata: the purchasing side can move 'horizontally' to talk to sales without first having to go 'vertically', through their own superiors in purchasing and up one hierarchical tree in order to go down another. Anyone can stop the works director to discuss a problem, and decisions are not made without the foreman being involved.

Fourth, job enrichment is pursued by trying to allow the workforce to control, as far as is practicable, the rhythms and structure of their working environment. Assembly lines have been reorganized in accordance with ideas put forward by the workforce who, for example, elected to work with a 'family' of machines (eg lathes) where they could retain their established working groups rather than mixing together milling machines and lathes under the same foremen.

On the assembly line one man now completely assembles a piece of switchgear from the first to the final stage instead of being a cog on the assembly line.

The company is also working towards a harmonization of practices such as sick pay and pension schemes for the shop floor and time off for visits to hospital and the dentist. Lateness penalties for the shop floor are being greatly reduced. White and blue collar eat the same meals in the same canteen, though there is still a separate directors' canteen on the same premises.

Behind all these reforms there is the dynamo of an incentive scheme. Roughly one-third of earnings spring from a payment-by-results system based on a price per piece for work submitted at the end of the week. But even here workers can opt either to work individually or collectively on payment by results. There is also provision within working groups either to work at a more tranquil pace, which older workers prefer, or flat out, which younger men with families tend to prefer.

Mr Chatterton sees his job as trying to get people to identify with the company by setting up a community spirit. This does not make the factory a paradise to work in but it has clearly reduced many of the tensions apparent in most factories and has resulted in gains for the company and for the workforce. Skilled operators earn about £120 a week, which is considered by unions and management to be a good wage for the area.

Mr Dan Outten, the chief convenor, agrees that community loyalty in the company is quite strong. He adds that, although this owes much to the personal style of the works director, he believes that if management elsewhere took the same attitude there would not be any problem.

Chapter 35
Profit improvement

Robert Heller wrote that 'businesses and managers don't earn profits, they earn money. Profit is an abstraction from the true, underlying movement of cash in and cash out.' It can be argued that profit is the result, not the objective, of efficient management.

On its own, profit, as shown on the balance sheet, is not necessarily an accurate measure of success in business. Profit figures can be 'influenced' by factors quite distinct from the trading performance of the company. These include how research and development is treated in the accounts, how stocks and work in progress are valued and how the flow of funds resulting from investments and realization of investments is dealt with. Rolls Royce is the classic example of a company whose profit figures proved to be misleading because of the way research and development expenditure was treated.

The president of International Harvester once said: 'All you have to do in business is to make some stuff and sell it to someone else for more than you paid for it.' And the controller of Bethlehem Steel stated: 'We're not in business to make steel, we're not in business to build ships, we're not in business to erect buildings. We're in business to make money.'

Both these statements are, of course, gross over-simplifications, but at least they emphasize the importance of the flow of money. Profit improvement is about increasing the flow of money into the business and reducing the flow of money out. It is not about maximizing an abstraction called 'profit' which is subject to so many extraneous influences. Perhaps we should think of it as performance improvement measured in financial terms rather than profit improvement. But profit improvement is what most people call it, and this is the term used here, with the reservations expressed above.

Factors affecting profit improvement

The three key factors are sales, costs and effectiveness.

Sales

The maximization of sales revenue depends first on good marketing. There are two approaches to marketing.

One is to assess the market in terms of what existing and potential customers will buy. This means an analysis of existing wants and buying patterns along with possible future needs. The other is to assess the scope for creating wants which do not exist at the moment, by developing and offering new products or services.

A company can maximize its market penetration by moving into market development (new markets for existing products), product development (improved or new products for existing markets), and diversification (new products for new markets).

Good marketing ensures that the company and its products are presented to customers by advertising, merchandising and public relations in a way which will best promote sales.

Finally, good marketing ensures that prices match what customers can be persuaded to pay, with the objective of maximizing contribution to profits and direct overheads. Maximizing profit means getting the right balance between high margins and high sales volume.

Sales depend on good marketing but do not necessarily follow from it. A well-trained, well-motivated and well-controlled sales force is an essential ingredient.

The final, but often neglected, ingredient is distribution. Effective marketing and selling will go for nought if order processing is inefficient, if the turn round of customer orders takes too long, if the wrong distribution channels are used from the point of view of speed, reliability and cost, or if customer queries and complaints are not dealt with properly.

Costs

One of the many wise things Peter Drucker has said is that: 'Cost, after all, does not exist by itself. It is always incurred — in intent at least — for the sake of a result. What matters therefore is not the absolute cost level but the rates between efforts and their results.'

The approach to cost reduction should therefore be to distinguish between those costs which are producing results and those which are not. Indiscriminate attacks on all costs — the 10 per cent slash approach — are counterproductive. On a selective basis, it may be better to cut something out altogether than to try and make a series of marginal cost reductions. As Drucker says: 'There is little point in trying to do cheaply what should not be done at all.'

Effectiveness
The objective should be effectiveness rather than just efficiency: to do the right things rather than merely to do things right.
  Effectiveness should be aimed for in the areas of:

☐ *Productivity* — getting more for less, whether it is manpower (output per head) capital (return on investment) or equipment (output per unit)
☐ *Finance* — tightening credit policies, cracking down on bad debts, controlling quantity and settlement discounts, optimizing cash holdings while gaining maximum interest on surplus cash and reducing interest payments on bank overdrafts to a minimum
☐ *Inventory* — keeping the amount tied up in working capital to the minimum consistent with the need to satisfy customer demand
☐ *Buying* — using supplier's warehouse space by 'calling off' at specified intervals, ensuring that competitive bids are obtained for all new or renewed contracts, specifying to buyers how they should use 'clout' to get good terms, resisting the temptation to over-order, having clearly laid down policies on mark-ups.

Approach to profit improvement

Profit improvement should be a continuous exercise. It should not be left until a crisis forces you to think about it. Start with an analysis of your current situation, using the checklist at the end of this chapter. Look at the whole product range for each market and assess the relative profitability and potential of all products and markets. Try to spot those which are fading and the up-and-coming ones. For fading products or markets, consider whether remedial or surgical treatment is appropriate. For up-and-coming products or markets work out how their progress can be assured and, possibly, accelerated.
  Use the 80/20 rule (Pareto's Law), to suggest the 20 per cent

of your products/markets which generate 80 per cent of your profits. Concentrate on maximizing the effectiveness of the 20 per cent of areas where the impact will be greatest.

Identify those factors within the business which are restraining its potential and, in Drucker's words, 'convert into opportunity what everybody else considers dangers'. Build on strengths rather than weaknesses.

Then look ahead. Project trends, anticipate problems and, where appropriate, innovate so that you can challenge the future rather than being overwhelmed by it.

Above all, bear in mind the results of the following highly pertinent research carried out by William Hall. Hall looked at 64 companies in depth to determine which had the best hopes of surviving in a hostile environment. Writing in the *Harvard Business Review* he identified two key factors. The best business survivors are, first, those which can deliver their products at the lowest cost, and/or second, those which have the 'highest differentiated position'. This means having the product which the customers perceive most clearly as being different and, in important respects, rather better than the competition.

Profit improvement checklist

Corporate analysis
1. Analyse result areas (divisions, markets, products) according to the revenue contribution they make and the costs they generate.
2. Assess for each product line or product in each market:
   a) The extent to which it is thriving, static or retracting
   b) Its potential for the future on the basis of different assumptions about the level of investment or cost necessary for development or survival.
3. Analyse corporate sales performance against plan and explain variances.
4. Analyse direct and overhead costs against plan and explain variances.
5. Assess development achievements (product and market) against plan and explain deviations.
6. Analyse key financial ratios (current and trends) and establish reasons for variations from the norm.
7. Conduct a zero-based budgeting exercise to assess the justification for all major expenditure.

8. Find the answers to three key questions:
   a) What business are we in?
   b) What business should we be in?
   c) What are we good at doing?
9. Assess corporate strengths and weaknesses in the fields of organization, management ability, calibre of staff, industrial relations, planning, development, marketing, selling, distribution, buying, inventory, financial base, productivity, production methods and facilities, use of new technology, including computers, management information and financial control.
10. Assess threats and opportunities:
    a) External, eg competition, government policies and interventions, market and product developments, inflation, exchange rates.
    b) Internal, eg staff, innovation, systems, financial resources (including cash flow).

Strategic plans

11. Prepare strategic plans which:
    a) Exploit opportunities and strengths revealed by the corporate analysis
    b) Are based on realistic assumptions and projections of future trends
    c) Take into account the cash required to finance expansion and product or market development.

Marketing

12. Find out everything possible about existing customers: buying habits, likes and dislikes, desire for changes or improvements to products or services.
13. Identify potential for getting new customers: what the company can do to meet existing needs or to create new wants.
14. Segment the market where this will reach different customers and can be profitable.
15. Penetrate new markets if this can be done profitably.
16. Check on cost effectiveness of advertising and promotional expenditure. Re-jig and expand advertising campaigns where it is confidently believed that this will improve results.
17. Pay more attention to merchandizing, eg advising retailers/agents on selling, holding special promotions, providing better point of sale material.

Product mix and development
18. Redistribute resources (finance, people, production and distribution) between products, as required to optimize returns on investment.
19. Maximize product profitability by:
    a) Cutting high risk, high capital projects
    b) Developing low cost, low risk products
    c) Cutting costs — advertising, promotion, packaging material, servicing or selling
    d) Reducing stockholding
    e) Reducing discounts
    f) Increasing prices.
20. Develop new products or services to meet defined market needs or to create new wants.
21. Eliminate unprofitable products or markets.

Sales
22. Improve the order-to-call ratio of sales representatives by better field supervision and training and more effective incentives.
23. Concentrate upon key accounts.
24. Eliminate unprofitable accounts.
25. Develop more high volume accounts.
26. Improve discount structure.
27. Provide incentives for customers to place larger orders or to remain loyal to the company's products.
28. Provide better support to sales representatives in the form of advertising, sales literature, merchandizing, and direct mail shots.
29. Speed response to customer enquiries.

Distribution
30. Analyse transport costs and switch to more economic methods.
31. Rationalize depot structure to speed deliveries and cut distribution and storage costs.
32. Use fewer, larger capacity vehicles and lengthen their life.
33. Introduce automatic handling methods wherever justified by the return on investment.
34. Make better use of storage space.

Production
35. Use quick sharp doses of method study to identify areas where output can be improved, eg eliminating bottlenecks,

illogical work flows, inefficient work scheduling.
36. Use value analysis techniques to reduce material costs.
37. Use group technology techniques to group associated processes into self-contained and easily controlled work units.
38. Rationalize product design so that more parts are interchangeable.
39. Ensure that procedures exist to relate customer orders and priorities to shop-floor capacity.
40. Improve shop-loading and production control techniques in order to smooth work flow, rationalize distribution of work, and eliminate delays because of shortages in materials, parts or tools.
41. Revise design standards and tolerances to match production facilities.
42. Reduce waste and scrap rates.
43. Increase machine utilization.
44. Introduce automation (mechanization) where justified by return on investment.

Buying
45. Use 'clout' to get better terms (but beware of placing orders which are too large).
46. Find alternative, cheaper or more reliable sources of supply.
47. Reserve capacity if there is a genuine and predictable need.
48. Place guaranteed orders in exchange for bulk prices.
49. Analyse for over-specification and reduce specifications to the minimum safe level.
50. Use 'call-off' system for regular supplies to cut storage costs.
51. Alter product design to allow for standard parts purchasing.

Inventory
52. Use economic order-quantity techniques to establish order points, taking into account inventory carrying charges, order preparation costs and demand for the item.
53. Use material requirements planning (MRP) techniques to ensure that the exact quantity of material wanted is on hand or is delivered not too long before it is required in accordance with sales demands.
54. Use computer modelling techniques to determine optimum stock levels, balancing the need to reduce working capital

with the need to avoid being out of stock.

55. Improve information on inventory so that action can be taken in good time to reduce stock to optimum levels.

Cost reduction

56. Look at the scope for cutting costs in all the major areas where expenses are incurred:
   a) Labour costs — look for overmanning, especially in indirect, service and staff departments
   b) Manufacturing costs — streamline production methods, reduce material costs
   c) Selling costs — advertising, promotions, public relations, packaging and display material
   d) Inventory — stock levels too high
   e) Operating — space, computers, services, plant and equipment.

57. Use zero-based budgeting and organization and methods techniques to analyse every activity not directly concerned with production. Establish the extent to which each is essential and the degree to which costs could be cut without making a significant impact on the productivity and efficiency of the business.

58. Reduce waste created by the company by eliminating:
   a) Unnecessary forms
   b) Over-complicated paperwork procedures
   c) Too many levels of management
   d) Delays in decision making because authority is not delegated down the line
   e) Bottlenecks and inefficient work flows.

59. Reduce waste created by staff, eg time wasting, absenteeism, extravagant use of the company's facilities and equipment.

Productivity

60. Extend or introduce a comprehensive method improvement programme.

61. Use work measurement to develop standards, give better control information and improve methods and procedures.

62. Introduce new technology, when justified, on a cost benefit basis.

63. Set productivity performance targets.

64. Buy out restrictive practices by productivity bargaining.

People
65. Identify effective managers and promote them.
66. Identify ineffective managers and remove them.
67. Introduce payment schemes which have a significant effect on motivation.
68. Encourage and train managers and supervisors to motivate their staff better.
69. Achieve better motivation by improving organization (more direct and immediate management) and the quality of working life. Get employees involved in productivity and quality improvement programmes.

Finance
70. Tighten credit policies.
71. Set priorities for capital expenditures.
72. Take steps to reduce bad debts.
73. Delay payments for as long as creditors will stand.
74. Analyse key ratios (eg profits as a percentage of sales and cash flow to current liabilities) and ensure that steps are taken to remedy adverse trends.
75. Ensure that management information, which allows proper control to be maintained over all aspects of the business, is available promptly.

Chapter 36

Report writing

The ability to express oneself clearly on paper and to write effective reports is one of a manager's most important skills. As often as not, it is through the medium of reports that you will convey your ideas and recommendations to your superiors and colleagues and inform them of the progress you are making.

What makes a good report?

The purpose of a report is to analyse and explain a situation, to propose and gain agreement to a plan. It should be logical, practical, persuasive and succinct.

To be an effective report writer you start by having something worthwhile to say. Clear thinking (Chapter 6) creative thinking (Chapter 12), problem solving (Chapter 23) and trouble shooting (Chapter 39) techniques will all help. Your analysis of opinions and facts and your evaluation of options should provide a base for positive conclusions and recommendations.

There are three fundamental rules for report writing:

☐ Give your report a logical structure
☐ Use plain words to convey your meaning
☐ Remember the importance of good, clear presentation of material.

Structure

A report should have a beginning, a middle and an end. If the report is lengthy or complex it will also need a summary of conclusions and recommendations. There may also be appendices containing detailed data and statistics.

Beginning
Your introduction should explain: why the report has been written, its aims, its terms of reference, and why it should be read. It should then state the sources of information upon which the report was based. Finally, if the report is divided into various sections, the arrangement and labelling of these sections should be explained.

Middle
The middle of the report should contain the facts you have assembled and your analysis of those facts. The analysis should lead logically to the conclusions and recommendations included in the final section. One of the most common weaknesses in reports is for the facts not to lead on naturally to the conclusions; the other is for the conclusions not to be supported by the facts.

Summarize the facts and your observations. If you have identified alternative courses of action, set out the pros and cons of each one, but make it quite clear which one you favour. Don't leave your readers in mid-air.

A typical trouble shooting report would start by describing the present situation; it would then list any problems or weaknesses in that situation, and proceed to explain why these have occurred.

End
The final section of the report should set out your recommendations, stating how each of them will help to achieve the stated aims of the report or overcome any weaknesses revealed by the analytical studies.

The benefits and costs of implementing the recommendations should then be explained. The next stage is to propose a method of proceeding – the programme of work, complete with deadlines and the names of people who would carry it out. Finally, tell the recipient(s) of the report what action, such as approval of plans or authorization of expenditure, you would like them to take.

Summary
In a long or complex report it is very helpful to provide a summary of conclusions and recommendations. It concentrates the reader's mind and can be used as an agenda in presenting and discussing the report. It is useful to cross-reference the

items to the relevant paragraphs or sections of the report.

Plain words

'If language is not correct, then what is said is not what is meant; if what is said is not what is meant, then what ought to be done remains undone.' (Confucius)

The heading of this section is taken from Sir Ernest Gower's *The Complete Plain Words*. This book is required reading for anyone interested in report writing. Gower's recommendations on how best to convey meaning without ambiguity, and without giving unnecessary trouble to the reader are:

1. Use no more words than are necessary to express your meaning, for if you use more you are likely to obscure it and to tire your reader. In particular do not use superfluous adjectives and adverbs, and do not use roundabout phrases where single words would serve.
2. Use familiar words rather than the far-fetched if they express your meaning equally well; for the familiar are more likely to be understood.
3. Use words with a precise meaning rather than those that are vague, for they will obviously serve better to make your meaning clear; and in particular, prefer concrete words to abstract for they are more likely to have a precise meaning.

You will not go far wrong if you follow these precepts.

Presentation

The way in which you present your report affects its impact and value. The reader should be able to follow your argument easily and not get bogged down in too much detail.

Paragraphs should be short and each one should be restricted to a single topic. If you want to list or highlight a series of points, tabulate them. For example:

Salary reviews
Control should be maintained over increments by issuing guidelines to managers on:

a) the maximum percentage increase to their pay roll allowable for increments to individual salaries;
b) the maximum percentage increase that should be paid to a member of staff.

Paragraphs should be numbered for ease of reference. Some people prefer the system which numbers main sections 1, 2, etc, sub-sections 1.1, 1.2, etc, and sub-sub-sections 1.1.1, 1.1.2, etc. However, this can be clumsy and distracting. A simpler system, which eases cross-referencing, is to number each paragraph, *not* the headings, 1, 2, 3, etc; sub-paragraphs or tabulations are identified as 1(a), 1(b), 1(c), etc and sub-sub-paragraphs if required as 1(a)(i), (ii), (iii) etc.

Use headings to guide people on what they are about to read and to help them find their way about the report. Main headings should be in capitals and sub-headings in lower-case.

A long report should have an index listing the main and sub-headings and their paragraph numbers like this:

	Paragraphs
SALARY ADMINISTRATION	83 — 92
Salary structure	84 — 88
Job evaluation	89 — 90
Salary reviews	91 — 92

In a shorter report it is often helpful to include a list of headings and paragraph numbers in the introduction.

Your report will make most impact if it is brief and to the point. Read and re-read your draft to cut out any superfluous material or flabby writing.

Do not clutter up the main pages of the report with masses of indigestible figures or other data. Summarize key statistics in compact easy-to-follow tables with clear headings. Relegate supporting material to an appendix.

Chapter 37
Team building

A manager spends much of his time leading teams and dealing with people in groups. Getting people to work well together is as important as motivating individuals.

Team building is a matter of establishing mutual confidence and trust among any group of people working for you. Your aim is to create a feeling of interdependence. A good team feels shared responsibility for getting results.

People do not necessarily work well together. Personal and inter-departmental rivalries exist in all organizations. Look out for them, they can ruin the most brilliant of schemes.

Take the example of a bright and brash young marketing executive imported by a British company to develop and market a new product. He had lots of ideas and all the qualities of initiative and drive that anyone could want in a development job. But he tended to ride rough-shod over the production, distribution and customer service departments. So far as he was concerned they were there to do as they were told. He dealt with them separately and never bothered to find out if there were any problems of coordination between them on matters relating to his product. As a result, the managers of these departments in more or less subtle ways sabotaged his efforts. They failed to get together on inter-departmental matters – partly because no one gave them a lead, and partly because there were rivalries and misunderstandings between them. Eventually, although the marketing concept was brilliant, the project failed, due to the refusal of the bright young executive to appreciate the importance of team building.

The company learnt its lesson. The next time an outsider was brought in to launch a new product, time was spent before he arrived to get a team together in the production, distribution and servicing divisions. They did the preliminary work setting up the project at their end, and were encouraged to feel that this was *their* project. As a result, when the new executive arrived, an atmosphere of enthusiasm and commitment existed. There was no problem in getting the team to work well together, especially as the new man was well aware of the need to build up a cohesive team.

Good teamwork is essential, but the existence of other highly cohesive groups is not necessarily a good thing for an organization. To become an effective team builder it is useful to know something about group behaviour and what makes an effective group.

How groups behave

Formal and informal groups
In the late twenties Elton Mayo conducted his first studies in group behaviour in the General Electric Hawthorne plant. He defined the two types of group that can exist within organizations:

☐ *Formal groups* set up by the organization to achieve a defined purpose which satisfies the organizational needs
☐ *Informal groups* set up by members of the organization because they have some affinity for one another. This type of group exists primarily to satisfy the needs of its members.

Informal groups may work for the organization, but they may work against it. For example, employees may get together to restrict output so that management will not tighten up a bonus scheme. In such a case the members of the group gang up against any 'ratebuster'.

Numerous investigations since Mayo's time have confirmed his observations. And you will find the same things happening today wherever people work together.

From management's point of view the advantages of well established informal groups are that they provide important extra channels of communication, promote teamwork and satisfy social needs that the organization or team leader cannot.

The disadvantages are that they may cut across the normal organizational channels and can develop norms or behaviour patterns in conflict with the aims of the leader.

The ideal situation is for formal and informal groupings to coincide, thus satisfying the needs of both the organization and the individuals in it.

227

Characteristics of established groups

The main characteristics of a well-established group (formal or informal) are as follows:

1. It is cohesive – the members of the group put up a united front to outsiders (who may include their boss or the management).
2. The members are interdependent – they rely upon each other for support in achieving both work and social goals.
3. It establishes its own norms or standards of behaviour which may influence members of the group to act in ways which are not in accordance with their own needs, or those of the organization, or those of the group leader.
4. The members of the group will tend to share beliefs and values (the group develops its own ideology) which may or may not be in accord with those of the organization or their boss.
5. The whole is greater than the sum of the parts, ie a well-knit group may exert greater influence when working as a whole than the total influence of each of its members if they were working separately.

One of the important things to look for in groups is the status system that may exist within them. If you understand the informal as well as the formal pecking order you will be better equipped to deal with problems within the team.

An interesting piece of research on status was carried out by William Whyte in the restaurant industry. Whyte points out that every work group has a status system. The various jobs into which the work of the group is subdivided have different prestige values in the eyes of the workers. The supervisor must know the status system of his group to cope effectively with problems of human relations.

Whyte's description of work groups in the kitchen of the Mammoth Restaurant illustrates the complex factors which determine an organized status system.

First, he observed that the work situations in the kitchen were socially ranked. At the top was the range where all the cooking was done. The most highly paid and most skilled positions were found at the range. Next came the salad station, which also dealt in finished foods of high prestige. Next in order of status were the chicken-preparation and meat-preparation stations. Toward the bottom of the hierarchy were the chicken-cooking and vegetable-preparation stations. At the very bottom was the fish station.

The larger stations had a status system of their own. For instance the vegetable-preparation station consisted of eight women. The tasks of the women in order of status were as follows: One and Two were the vegetable cooks; Three divided her time between cooking and preparing vegetables; Four was in charge of preparation under the direction of One and occasionally did some cooking; Five, Six, Seven and Eight did no cooking. This status pattern had developed as a result of the formally specified division of labour (eg cooking duties versus non-cooking duties) and personal factors. (Seven and Eight were older women who worked sitting down, thus giving the younger workers the opportunity to organize and direct the work.)

Status influenced the assignment of different vegetables to the women; for vegetables, it seems, differ markedly in social standing. Such decorative or luxury vegetables as parsley, chives and celery are at the top. Green beans head the regular vegetables, followed by spinach and carrots. Next to the bottom are potatoes. Onions are considered the most undesirable of all because of their odour.

Higher-status workers tended to work on higher-status vegetables. When all the women were working on the same vegetable, the higher-status workers handled later stages in the process of preparation (eg dicing carrots instead of scraping them). This brought them closer to the social pinnacle of the kitchen — the range — and put them in a position to criticize the work of the earlier stages.

The working supervisor of the fish station was one of the most skilled and valuable workers in the kitchen. Yet her station stood at the bottom of the status hierarchy because the other workers considered the fish station a smelly, dirty, and unpleasant place to work.

Effective teams

An effective team is cohesive, self-supportive and knows where it is going. Douglas McGregor described the main features which indicate such a team:

1. The atmosphere tends to be informal, comfortable, relaxed.
2. There is a lot of discussion in which initially everyone participates, but it remains pertinent to the task of the group.

3. The task or objective of the group is well understood and accepted by the members. There will have been free discussion of the objective at some point until it was formulated in such a way that the members of the group could commit themselves to it.
4. The members listen to each other. Every idea is given a hearing. People do not appear to be afraid of looking foolish by putting forward a creative thought, even if it seems fairly extreme.
5. There is disagreement. Disagreements are not suppressed or overriden by premature group action. The reasons are carefully examined, and the group seeks to resolve them rather than to dominate the dissenter.
6. Most decisions are reached by a kind of consensus in which it is clear that everybody is in general agreement and willing to go along.
7. Criticism is frequent, frank, and relatively comfortable. There is little evidence of personal attack, either openly or in a hidden fashion.
8. People are free in expressing their feelings as well as their ideas both on the problem and on the group's operation.
9. When action is taken, clear assignments are made and accepted.
10. The leader of the group does not dominate it, nor does the group defer unduly to him.

These characteristics present an ideal which you might strive for but will seldom attain. There will be times when you have to do away with some of the more time consuming ones, such as 2, 6, and 8 and concentrate on 3 and 9: 'The task or objective of the group is well understood and accepted by the members . . . when action is taken, clear assignments are made and accepted.'

Leadership
As the team leader you are responsible for seeing that it displays as many of the above characteristics as are appropriate to the situation. The role of the leader is critical, especially in times of crisis, when the group must get into action fast. Robert Hamblin of the University of Michigan carried out an interesting laboratory investigation into the effects of a crisis upon team leaders.

In his experiment college students, divided into 24 groups of three, were asked to play a modified shuffleboard game for about 30 minutes. They were told to learn the special rules of the game by trying out different procedures. A red light would flash every time a rule was violated; a green light every time a score was made.

The game was presented to the students as a test of their ability to analyse a rather complex situation. The groups were told they were in competition with high school students who had earlier participated in a similar experiment and that comparative cumulative scores would be posted at the end of each of the game's six five-minute playing periods.

Each time a player suggested a procedure for testing a rule or suggested a possible rule, he was given an 'influence-attempt score'. If the attempted suggestion was adopted by the group, he was given an 'accepted influence score'. Two measures were then calculated for each player for each playing period: the influence ratio and an acceptance rate. The influence ratio was the number of influence-attempt scores of each divided by the average influence-attempt scores of the other two group members. The acceptance rate was the proportion of a subject's influence attempts which were accepted.

By the end of the first three playing periods, the average group had learned most of the rules of the game and was enjoying a comfortable, albeit fictitious, lead over the high school competitors. In the fourth playing period, twelve of the groups were exposed to a 'crisis' — an unannounced change in the rules was made. Procedures that had been legal were now made illegal and vice versa. As soon as the players learned a new rule, it was again changed. The members of the crisis groups were unable to make a single score during the last three periods. The remaining twelve groups (control groups) continued to play under the original rules.

The results indicated two things. First, leaders have more influence at a time of crisis. The members of a group accept leadership when faced with a crisis. Second, a group rejects its old leader and replaces him if the old leader does not quickly and decisively meet the crisis. Whereas nine of the twelve crisis groups replaced their original leaders, only three of the control groups, did so.

Getting cooperation
The members of an effective team cooperate equally well with one another and with their team leader.

Elton Mayo and many other investigators of teamwork have

demonstrated that the manager can exert considerable, if indirect, influence by simply showing interest in how the team operates and getting involved with its members. In his Hawthorne studies Mayo showed that the output of some of the teams of girls he was studying increased just because the investigators were taking an interest in them:

> By asking for their help and cooperation the investigators had made the girls feel important. Their whole attitude had changed from that of separate cogs in a machine to that of a congenial group trying to help the company solve a problem. They had found stability, a place where they belonged and work whose purpose they could clearly see. And so they worked faster and better than they ever had in their lives.

Team building methods

To build an effective team, exercise your leadership skills. It is particularly important for you to demonstrate to your team that:

☐ You know where you want them to go
☐ You know how they are going to get there
☐ You know what you expect each member of the team to achieve
☐ You know what you are doing.

Such an approach to leadership provides a firm base which will allow you to concentrate on doing the following things:

1. Encourage participation in agreeing objectives and targets
2. Group related tasks together so that group members know that they can make their jobs easier by cooperating with others
3. Rotate jobs within groups so that group members identify with the team as a whole rather than with their own jobs
4. Ensure that communications flow freely within and between groups
5. Encourage informal meetings between groups to resolve problems.

Chapter 38

Time management

I wasted time, now doth time waste me (*Richard II*).

If you were told by your chairman that he wanted you for a special assignment which would mean working directly under him, give you the opportunity to deal with strategic issues, broaden your experience and provide you with excellent promotion prospects, would you take it? The answer would, of course, be yes. If, however, you were told that you would spend one day a week on this assignment and carry out your present duties in the remaining four days, would you still accept the job? Of course you would. But you would be admitting that you could, if you organized yourself better, do your existing work in four-fifths of the time you spend at the moment.

To recover that one-fifth or more, you need to think systematically about how you use your time. You can then take steps to organize yourself better and to get other people to help or at least not to hinder you.

Analysis

The first thing to do is to find out where there is scope for improving your use of time.

Your job
Start with your job — the tasks you have to carry out and the objectives you are there to achieve. Try and establish an order of priority between your tasks and among your objectives.

It is more difficult to do this if you have a number of potentially conflicting areas of responsibility. A good example of this was a director of administration who had a ragbag of responsibilities including property, office services and staff.

He had perpetual problems with conflicting priorities and, all too frequently, at the end of the day he would say to himself: 'I have wasted my time, I have achieved next to nothing.'

He took a day off to think things through and realized that he had to take a broad view before getting into detail. He felt that if he could sort out the relative importance of his objectives he would be in a better position to attach priorities to his tasks. He quickly realized that, as an administrator, his first objective was to set up and maintain systems which would run smoothly. Having done this, he could rely on preventive maintenance to reduce problems. But when a crisis did occur — which was inevitable in his area — he could concentrate on fire-fighting in one place without having to worry about what was going on elsewhere.

His second objective, therefore, was to give himself sufficient free time to concentrate on major problems so that he could react swiftly to them. He then classified the sort of issues that could arise and decided which could safely be delegated to others and which he should deal with himself. He was thus prepared to allocate priorities as the problems landed on his desk and to select the serious ones to deal with himself, knowing that the administrative system would go on without interruption.

How you spend your time

Having sorted out your main priorities you should analyse in more detail how you spend your time. This will identify time-consuming activities and indicate where there are problems as well as possible solutions to them.

The best way to analyse time is to keep a diary. Do this for a week, or preferably two to three, as one week may not provide a typical picture. Divide the day into 15-minute sections and note down what you did in each period. Against each space, summarize how effectively you spent your time by writing V for valuable, D for doubtful and U for useless. If you want to make more refined judgements give your ratings plusses or minuses. For example:

Time	Task	Rating
9.00 – 9.15	Dealt with incoming mail	V
9.15 – 9.30	Dealt with incoming mail	V
9.30 – 9.45	Discussed admin problem	D
9.45 – 10.00	Discussed admin problem	D
10.00 – 10.15	Deputized at meeting	U
10.15 – 10.30	Deputized at meeting	U
10.30 – 10.45	Deputized at meeting	U
10.45 – 11.00	Deputized at meeting	U

At the end of the week analyse your time under the following headings:

☐ Reading
☐ Writing
☐ Dictating
☐ Telephoning
☐ Dealing with people (individuals or groups)
☐ Attending meetings
☐ Travelling
☐ Other (specify).

Analyse also the VDU ratings of the worth of each activity under each heading.

This analysis will provide you with the information you need to spot any weaknesses in the way in which you manage time. Use the time-consumer's checklist at the end of this chapter to identify problems and possible remedies.

Organizing yourself

Such an analysis will usually throw up weaknesses in the way you plan your work and establish your priorities. You have to fit the tasks you must complete into the time available to complete them, and get them done in order of importance.

Some people find it difficult, if not impossible, to plan their work ahead. They find that they work best if they have to achieve almost impossible deadlines. Working under pressure concentrates the mind wonderfully, they say. Journalists are a case in point.

But ordinary mortals, who work under a variety of conflicting pressures, cannot rely upon crisis action to get them out of log-jams of work. For most of us it is better to try and minimize the need for working under exceptional pressure by a little attention to the organization of our week or day. At the very least you should use your diary for long-range planning, organize your weekly activities in broad outline and plan each day in some detail.

Use of your diary

Attempt to leave at least one day a week free of meetings and avoid filling any day with appointments. In other words leave blocks of unallocated time for planning, thinking, reading, writing and dealing with the unexpected.

Weekly organizer

Sit down at the beginning of each week with your diary and plan how you are going to spend your time. Assess each of your projects or tasks and work out priorities. Leave blocks of time for dealing with correspondence and seeing people. Try to preserve one free day, or at least half a day, if it is at all possible.

If it helps you to put everything down on paper, draw up a simple weekly organizer form and record what you intend to do each morning, afternoon and, if it's work, evening.

Daily organizer

At the beginning of each day, consult your diary to check on your plans and commitments. Refer to the previous day's organizer to find out what is outstanding. Inspect your pending tray and in-tray to check on what remains and what has just arrived.

Then write down the things to do:

1. Meetings or interviews
2. Telephone calls
3. Tasks in order of priority:
   A – must be done today
   B – ideally should be done today but could be left till tomorrow
   C – can be dealt with later.

Plan broadly when you are going to fit your A and B priority tasks into the day. Tick off your tasks as they have been completed. Retain the list to consult next day.

You do not need an elaborate form for this purpose. Many successful time managers use a blank sheet of paper, but a simple form which you can use, is shown overleaf.

DAILY ORGANIZER   Date . . . .

Meetings and appointments

Committee/person	Where	When

To telephone

Person	About what	When

To do

Tasks *(in order of priority)*	Priority rating* A, B or C	Approximate timing

* A = must be done today. B = ideally done today. C = later.

Organizing other people

Your first task is to organize yourself, but other people can
help, if you can guide and encourage them. They include your
secretary, boss, colleagues, subordinates and outside contacts.

Your secretary

A secretary can be a great help: sorting incoming mail into what
needs immediate attention and what can be looked at later;
managing appointments within your guidelines; keeping
unwanted callers at bay; intercepting telephone calls; dealing
with routine or even semi-routine correspondence; sorting and
arranging your papers and the filing system for easy accessi-
bility; getting people on the telephone for you and so on. The
list is almost endless. Every efficient boss will recognize that he
depends a lot on an efficient secretary.

Your boss

Your boss can waste your time with over-long meetings, needless
interruptions, trivial requests and general nitpicking. Maybe
there is nothing you can do about him. But you can learn how
to avoid doing the same to your own staff.

On your own behalf you can cultivate the polite art of cutting short tedious discussions. Such formulas as, 'I hope you feel we have cleared up this problem — I'll get out of your hair now and get things moving' are useful. And you might be able, subtly, to indicate that he is going to get better performance from you if he leaves you alone. It's difficult but it's worth trying.

Your colleagues
Try to educate them to avoid unnecessary interruptions. Don't anger them by shutting them out when they have something urgent to discuss. But if it can wait, get them to agree to meet you later at a fixed time. Try to avoid indulging in too many pleasantries over the telephone. Be brisk but not brusque.

Your subordinates
You will save a lot of time with your subordinates if you systematically decide what work you can delegate to them. You save even more time if you delegate clearly and spell out how and when you want them to report back.

An 'open door' policy is fine in theory but time-wasting in practice. Learn to say no to subordinates who want to see you when you are engaged on more important business. But always give them a time when they can see you and stick to it.

Talking generally to your staff about their job and outside interests can be time well spent if it helps to increase mutual understanding and respect. Allow for this in your schedule and be prepared to extend business discussions into broader matters when the opportunity arises. But don't overdo it.

Outside contacts
The same rules apply to outside contacts. Prevent them from seeing you without an appointment. Ask your secretary to block unwanted telephone calls. Brief your contacts on what you expect from them and when meetings should be arranged.

Time-consumer's checklist

Problem	Possible remedies
TASKS	
1. Work piling up	☐ Set priorities
	☐ Set deadlines
	☐ Make realistic time estimates — most people underestimate — add 20 per cent to your first guess.

Problem	*Possible remedies*
2. Trying to do too much at once	☐ Set priorities ☐ Do one thing at a time ☐ Learn to say no to yourself as well as other people.
3. Getting involved in too much detail	☐ Delegate more.
4. Postponing unpleasant tasks	☐ Set a timetable and stick to it ☐ Get unpleasant tasks over with quickly — you will feel better afterwards.
5. Insufficient time to think	☐ Reserve blocks of time — part of a day or week — for thinking. No paperwork, no interruptions.

PEOPLE

6. Constant interruptions from people calling into your office	☐ Use secretary to keep unwanted visitors out ☐ Make appointments and see that people stick to them ☐ Reserve block times when you are not to be interrupted.
7. Constant telephone interruptions	☐ Get your secretary to intercept and, where appropriate, divert calls ☐ State firmly that you will call back when convenient.
8. Too much time spent in conversation	☐ Decide in advance what you want to achieve when you meet someone, and keep pleasantries to a minimum at the beginning and end ☐ Concentrate on keeping yourself and the other person to the point — it is too easy to divert or be diverted ☐ Learn how to end meetings quickly but not too brusquely.

PAPERWORK

9. Flooded with incoming paper	☐ Get your secretary to sort it into three folders: action now, action later, information ☐ Take yourself off the circulation list of useless information ☐ Only ask for written memos and reports when you really need them ☐ Encourage people to present information and reports clearly and succinctly ☐ Ask for summaries rather than the whole report ☐ Take a course in rapid reading.

Problem	*Possible remedies*
10. Too many letters/memos to write or dictate	☐ Use the telephone more ☐ Avoid individually typed acknowledgements ☐ Practise writing a succinct 'yes/no/ let's talk' on the memos you receive and return them to the sender.
11. Paperwork piling up	☐ Do it now ☐ Set aside the first half hour or so in the day to deal with urgent correspondence ☐ Leave a period at the end of the day for less urgent reading ☐ Aim to clear at least 90 per cent of the paper on your desk every day.
12. Lost or mislaid papers	☐ Arrange, or get your secretary to organize, papers on current projects in separate easily accessible folders ☐ Don't hang on to papers in your pending tray – clear it daily ☐ Set up a filing and retrieval system which will enable you to get at papers easily ☐ Ensure that your secretary keeps a day book of correspondence as a last resort method of turning up papers ☐ Keep a tidy desk.

MEETINGS

Problem	*Possible remedies*
13. Too much time spent in meetings	☐ If you set up the meeting: avoid regular meetings when there is nothing that needs saying regularly, review all the meetings you hold and eliminate as many as you can ☐ Get yourself taken off committees if your presence is not essential or if someone else is more appropriate ☐ As chairman: set limits for the duration of meetings and keep to them, cut out waffle and repetition, allow discussion but insist on making progress, have a logical agenda and stick to it ☐ As a member: don't waffle, don't talk for the sake of talking, don't waste time scoring points or boosting your ego.

Problem	*Possible remedies*

TRAVELLING

14. Too much time spent on travelling

- ☐ Use the phone or post
- ☐ Send someone else
- ☐ Ask yourself, every time you plan to go anywhere, 'is my journey really necessary?'
- ☐ Plan the quickest way – air, rail or car.

Chapter 39

Trouble shooting

No matter what you do, things will sometimes go wrong. As a manager, you will often be called upon to put them right, or to employ other people to do it for you.

Trouble shooting requires diagnostic ability, to size up the difficulties; know-how, to select the required solution and decide how to implement it; and managerial skill, to put the solution into effect. It can be divided into three main parts:

☐ Planning the campaign
☐ Diagnosis
☐ Cure.

Planning the campaign

Even if you decide to do it yourself without using management consultants, you can still take a leaf out of the consultant's book. A good management consultant will go through the following stages:

☐ Analysis of the present situation — what has happened and why
☐ Development of alternative solutions to the problem
☐ Decision as to the preferred solution, stating the costs and benefits of implementing it
☐ Defining a method of proceeding — how and over what timescale should the solution be implemented, who does it and with what resources. If a staged implementation is preferred, the stages will be defined and a programme worked out.

The most important thing to do at the planning stage is to define the problem, clarify objectives and terms of reference. A problem defined is a problem half solved. And it is the difficult half. The rest should follow quite naturally if an analytical approach is adopted.

Once you know what the problem is you can define what you want done and prepare terms of reference for those who are conducting the investigation, including yourself. These should set out the problem, how and by whom it is to be tackled, what is to be achieved and by when. All those concerned in the exercise should know what these terms of reference are.

The next step is to programme the trouble shooting assignment. Four things need to be decided: the information you need, where you get it from, how you obtain it and who gets it. Draw up lists of facts required and the people who can supply them. Remember you will have to deal with opinion as well as fact; all data are subject to interpretation. List those who are likely to understand what has happened and why. Those who might have good ideas about what to do next.

Then draw up your programme. Give notice that you require information. Warn people in plenty of time that you want to discuss particular points with them and that you expect them to have thought about the subject *and* have supporting evidence to hand.

Diagnosis

Diagnosis means finding out *what* is happening — the symptom — and then digging to establish *why* it is happening — the cause. There may be a mass of evidence. The skilled diagnostician dissects the facts, sorts out what is relevant to the problem and refines it all down until he reveals the crucial pieces of information which show the cause of the problem and point to its solution.

Analytical ability — being able to sort the wheat from the chaff — is a key element in diagnosis. It is a matter of getting the facts and then submitting each one to a critical examination, in order to determine which is significant.

During the process of diagnosis you must remain open-minded. You should not allow yourself to have preconceptions or to be over-influenced by anyone's opinion. Listen and observe, but suspend judgement until you can range all the facts against all the opinions.

At the same time, do whatever you can to enlist the interest and support of those involved. If you can minimize their natural fears and suspicions, those close to the problem will reveal ideas and facts which might otherwise be concealed from you.

Trouble shooting checklist

Base your diagnosis on an analysis of the factors likely to have contributed to the problem: people, systems, structure and circumstances.

People

1. Have mistakes been made? If so, why? Is it because staff are inadequate in themselves or is it because they have been badly managed or trained?
2. If management is at fault, was the problem one of system, structure or the managers themselves?
3. If the people doing the job are inadequate why were they selected in the first place?

Systems

4. To what extent are poor systems or procedures to blame for the problem?
5. Is the fault in the systems themselves? Are they badly designed or inappropriate?
6. Or is it the fault of the people who operate or manage the systems?

Structure

7. How far has the organization or management structure contributed to the problem?
8. Do people know what is expected of them?
9. Are activities grouped together logically, so that adequate control can be exercised over them?
10. Are managers and supervisors clear about their responsibilities for maintaining control and do they exercise these responsibilities effectively?

Circumstances

11. To what extent, if any, is the problem a result of circumstances beyond the control of those concerned? For example, have external economic pressures or changing government policies had a detrimental effect?

12. If there have been external pressures, has there been a
failure to anticipate or to react quickly enough to them?
13. Have adequate resources (people, money and materials)
been made available, and if not, why not?

Cure

The diagnosis should point the way to the cure. But this may
still mean that you have to evaluate different ways of dealing
with the problem. There is seldom 'one best way', only a choice
between alternatives. You have to narrow them down until you
reach the one which, *on balance*, is better than the others.

Your diagnosis should have established the extent to which
the problem is one of people, systems, structure or circumstances. Fallible human beings may well be at the bottom of it.
If so remember not to indulge in indiscriminate criticism. Your
job is to be constructive; to build people up, not to destroy
them.

Avoid being too theoretical. Take account of circumstances
– including the ability of the people available now to deal
with the problem, or, if you have doubts, the availability of
people from elsewhere who can be deployed effectively. Your
recommendation should be practical in the sense that it can be
made to work with resources which are readily available and
within acceptable timescales.

You must make clear not only what needs to be done but
how it is to be done. Assess costs as well as benefits and
demonstrate that the benefits outweigh the costs. Resources
have to be allocated, a timescale set and, above all, specific
responsibility given to people to get the work done. Your
recommendations have to be realistic in the sense that they can
be phased in without undue disruption and without spending
more time and money than is justified by the results.

Take care when you apportion blame to individuals. Some
may clearly be inadequate and have to be replaced. Others
may be the victims of poor management, poor training or
circumstances beyond their control. Their help may be essential
in overcoming the trouble. It is unwise to destroy their
confidence or their willingness to help.

Using management consultants

A management consultant has been described, or dismissed, as a man with a briefcase fifty miles from home. Robert Townsend has suggested that consultants are people 'who borrow your watch to tell you what time it is and then walk off with it'.

Calling in consultants in desperation can indeed be an expensive and time wasting exercise. But they have their uses. They bring experience and expertise in diagnosis. They can act as an extra pair of hands when suitable people are not available from within the organization. And, as a third party, they can sometimes see the wood through the trees and unlock ideas within the company which, sadly, are often inhibited by structural or managerial constraints.

There are, however, a number of rules which you should be aware of when contemplating bringing in consultants.

DO	*DON'T*
Get tenders from two or three firms and compare, not only their fees, but their understanding of your problem and the practical suggestions they have on how to tackle it.	Be bamboozled by a smooth principal who is employed mainly as a salesman.
Check on the experience of the firm *and*, most importantly, of the consultant who is going to carry out the assignment.	Go for a big firm simply because it has a good reputation. It may not have the particular expertise you want.
Brief the firm very carefully on the terms of reference.	Accept any old consultant that comes along. Many redundant executives have set up as consultants without having a clue about how to do it. There is a lot of skill in being an effective consultant. Check that the firm is a member of the Management Consultants Association or that the principal is a member of the Institute of Management Consultants (for UK-based firms). These provide a guarantee of professional status.
Get a clear statement of the proposed programme, total estimated costs (fees *plus* expenses) and who is actually going to carry out the assignment.	
Meet and assess the consultant who is going to do the work.	Allow the consultant to change programme without prior consultation.
Insist on regular progress meetings.	Leave the consultant to his own devices for too long. Keep in touch. Appoint a member of your staff to liaise or even to work with him.
Ensure that the outcome of the assignment is a practical proposal which you can implement yourself, or with the minimum of further help.	

Bibliography

This bibliography first lists the main references, chapter by chapter. A further list then provides a selection of general texts on management.
** indicates those books which are regarded by the writer as essential reading.
* indicates books which are particularly interesting.

Introduction

Hooper, Sir Frederick *Management Survey*, Penguin Books, Harmondsworth, 1960.
Stewart, Rosemary *The Reality of Management*,** Heinemann, London, 1963.

Chapter 1

McClelland, David C. *The Achieving Society*, Van Nostrand, New York, 1961.
McGregor, Douglas *The Human Side of Enterprise*,** McGraw-Hill, New York, 1960.
Townsend, Robert *Up the Organization*,** Michael Joseph, London, 1970.

Chapter 2

Drucker, Peter *The Practice of Management*,** Heinemann, London, 1955.
Levinson, Harry 'Appraisal of what performance?' *Harvard Business Review*, July-August 1976.

Chapter 4

Heller, Robert *The Business of Success*,* Barrie & Jenkins, London, 1982.
Heller, Robert *The Naked Manager*,** Barrie & Jenkins, London, 1972.

Chapter 5

Sloan, Alfred P. Jnr *My Years With General Motors*, Pan Books, London, 1967.
Woodward, Joan 'Resistance to change', *Management International Review*, Vol. 8, 1968.

Chapter 6

De Bono, Edward *Lateral Thinking for Managers*,* McGraw-Hill, London, 1971.
Stebbing, L. Susan *Thinking to Some Purpose*,* Penguin Books, Harmondsworth, 1959.

Chapter 8

Follett, Mary Parker *Creative Experience*,* Longmans Green, New York, 1924.

Chapter 9

Taylor, F. W. *Principles of Scientific Management*, Harper, New York, 1911.

Chapter 10

Carlson, Sune *Executive Behavior: A Study of the Work Load and the Working Methods of Managing Directors*, Strombergs, Stockholm, 1951.
Urwick, L. F. *The Elements of Administration*, Pitman, London, 1947.

Chapter 12

Koestler, Arthur *The Act of Creation*, Hutchinson, London, 1964.

Chapter 15

Reddin, W. J. *Managerial Effectiveness*, McGraw-Hill, London, 1970.

Chapter 20

Adair, John *Action Centered Leadership*,* McGraw-Hill, London, 1973.
Halpin, A. W. and Winer, B. J. *A Factorial Study of the Leader Behavior Description*, Ohio State University, 1957.
Jay, Antony *Management and Machiavelli*,** Hodder & Stoughton, London, 1967.

Chapter 21

Tannenbaum, R. and Schmidt, W. H. 'How to choose a leadership pattern',** *Harvard Business Review*, May-June 1973.

Chapter 23

Parkinson, C. Northcote *Parkinson's Law*,** Murray, London, 1958.

Chapter 24

Herzberg, Fredrick *The motivation-hygiene theory*,** Management and Motivation, (eds. Vroom and Deci), Penguin Books, Harmondsworth, 1970.
Lawler, E. E. and Porter, L. *Antecedent attitudes of effective managerial performance*,* Management and Motivation, (eds. Vroom and Deci), Penguin Books, Harmondsworth, 1970.
Maslow, A. H. *A theory of human motivation*,** Management and Motivation, (eds. Vroom and Deci), Penguin Books, Harmondsworth, 1970.
Vroom, Victor H. *The nature of the relationship between motivation and performance*,** Management and Motivation, (eds. Vroom and Deci), Penguin Books, Harmondsworth, 1970.

Chapter 27

Burns, T. and Stalker, G. M. *Management of Innovation*,* Tavistock, London, 1957.
Croome, Honor *Human Problems of Innovation*,* Problems of Progress in Industry, No 5, HMSO, 1960.

Chapter 31

Kotter, John P. 'Power, dependence and effective management',* *Harvard Business Review*, July-August 1971.
McClelland, David C. and Burnham, David H. 'Power is the great motivator',* *Harvard Business Review*, March-April 1976.

Chapter 35

Hall, William K. 'Survival strategies in a hostile environment',* *Harvard Business Review*, September-October 1980.

Chapter 36

Gowers, Sir Ernest *The Complete Plain Words*,** HMSO, 1977.

Chapter 37

Hamblin, Robert *Leadership and Crisis*, Sociometry, New York, 1958.
Mayo, Elton *Social Problems of an Industrial Civilization*, Harvard University Press, Cambridge, Massachusetts, 1945.
Whyte, W. F. *Human Relations in the Restaurant Industry*, McGraw-Hill, New York, 1948.

General texts on management

Brech, E. F. L. *The Principles and Practice of Management*,* Longman, London, 1975.
Child, John *Organization: A Guide to Problems and Practice*,* Harper & Row, London, 1977.
Dale, Ernest *Management Theory and Practice*,* McGraw-Hill, New York, 1978.
Drucker, Peter *The Effective Executive*,** Heinemann, London, 1962.
Drucker, Peter *Managing for Results*,* Heinemann, London, 1963.

Drucker, Peter *Managing in Turbulent Times*,* Heinemann, London, 1963.

Falk, Roger *The Business of Management: Art or Craft*,* Penguin Books, Harmondsworth, 1976.

Handy, Charles B. *The Gods of Management: How They Work and Why They Will Fail*,* Souvenir Press, London, 1978.

Handy, Charles B. *Understanding Organizations*,** Penguin Books, Harmondsworth, 1982.

Hickson, Ronald W. *How to be a Successful Manager*,** Thorsons Publishing Group, Wellingborough, 1978.

Koontz, H., O'Donnell, C. and Weinrich, H. *Management*,* McGraw-Hill, New York, 1980.

Moore, Franklin, G. *Management*,* Harper & Row, New York, 1964.